# Overworked AND Underpaid

How to Go From Being a Low-Paid Secretary to Being a High-Paid Secretary to Having Your Own Secretary

## MARY BRIDGET CARROLL

Fawcett Columbine • New York

A Fawcett Columbine Book
Published by Ballantine Books
Copyright ©1983 by St. Robert's Press, Inc.

Library of Congress Catalog Card Number: 84-90845

ISBN: 0-449-90132-7

## PICTURE CREDITS

The author wishes to thank the following individuals and organizations for their kind permission to reproduce the copyrighted pictures in this book.

Culver Pictures pages 32, 33, 34, 35, 36, 37, 38 and 43 (top). CBS Entertainment—186, 187 (bottom) 188, 189 and 190 (top). World Wide—44 (bottom). United Press International, Inc.—44 (top). 187 (top) and 196. From the Twentieth Century-Fox release "Three Coins In The Fountain" ©1954 Twentieth Century-Fox Film Corporation, all rights reserved—192 (top). From the Twentieth Century-Fox release "Nine To Five" ©1980 Twentieth Century-Fox Corporation, all rights reserved—193 (bottom). From the Twentieth Century-Fox television series "Nine To Five" ©1983 Twentieth Century-Fox Film corporation, all rights reserved—190 (bottom). Reprinted by permission: Tribune Company Syndicate, Inc.—185, 194 (top) and 195 (top). King Features—185, 194 (bottom) and 195 (bottom). Paramount Pictures Corporation "Saturday Night Fever"—193 (top). From the motion picture "Psycho" (Universal, 1960), courtesy of Universal Pictures—192 (bottom). Courtesy of RKO General Pictures—191. Courtesy of the Rosen family—39. J.J. Donnelly—197. Ozalid Corp., Mahwah, NJ. Division of Aarque Office Systems, Inc.—42 (top). New York Public Library Picture Collection—41 (top). GF Furniture Systems, Youngstown, Ohio—42 (bottom). Shaw-Walker Co.—41 (bottom). Reprinted with permission from Esquire (October 1950). ©1950 by Esquire Associates—40. Drawing by Whitney Darrow, Jr.; ©1954, 1982 The New Yorker Magazine, Inc.—43 (bottom). Honeywell—45 (bottom). Philip Morris Incorporated—44 (top).

First Ballantine Books Edition: September 1984

10  9  8  7  6  5  4  3  2  1

**BEWARE**

Never buy a How-To-Get-A-Job book that's
dedicated to a guru, a maharishi or somebody
who found God after legally changing his name.

*This book is dedicated
to secretaries
who realize that if
you can survive being
a secretary — you can
survive anything.*

# ACKNOWLEDGEMENTS

Without Bob Donnelly's ideas and professional writing skills, Overworked and Underpaid could not have happened. This is his book, too.

My family for their continual love and support.

Marie Donnelly and Patricia Byer who were the secretaries behind this book on secretaries.

Mike Wollman for his art direction.

Russell Pierce for his design consultation and illustrations.

Terry Beatty for the cartoon illustrations.

Ken Bruzenak for lettering.

Jennifer Donnelly and Robert V. Kelly for additional illustrations.

Jeff McCartney and Joe Papaleo for proofreading.

Jan Mullaney and Bruce Palley—my comic book mavens.

Tim Nero at Zero Hour Graphics for his dedication and understanding.

Professional Secretaries International, 9 to 5 The Bureau of Labor Statistics and the Administrative Management Society.

Paul Mifsud for his contribution on "The ABCs of Office Computers."

The Rock Music Sourcebook by Bob Macken, Peter Fornatale and Bill Ayres for song titles.

Many of the slogans that appear throughout the book are used with the permission of Image Designs (T-shirts).

To countless others who made this book possible but especially to Joe Fisher—*sine qua non*.

# CONTENTS

PREFACE ............................................................................. 13

CHAPTER 1 ....................................................................... 19
HOW TO FIND A $250,000 A YEAR JOB BY READING
THIS BOOK (...AND OTHER RIDICULOUS MYTHS AND
LIES PERPETRATED BY HOW TO FIND A JOB BOOKS)

CHAPTER 2 ....................................................................... 24
WHO IS MARY BRIDGET CARROLL AND WHY IS SHE
SAYING ALL OF THOSE TERRIBLE THINGS ABOUT
EVERYONE?

CHAPTER 3 ....................................................................... 32
ONE HUNDRED YEARS OF SECRETARIES:
A PICTORIAL ESSAY

CHAPTER 4 ....................................................................... 46
20 THINGS (GIVE OR TAKE A FEW) YOU CAN DO TO
GET YOUR FOOT OUT OF YOUR MOUTH AND INTO
THE DOOR OF A GREAT JOB

CHAPTER 5 ....................................................................... 53
THE RÉSUMÉ (A BRIEF COURSE IN CREATIVE
WRITING)

CHAPTER 6 ....................................................................... 65
DRESS LIKE A LOW-PAID SECRETARY AND YOU'LL
ALWAYS BE TREATED LIKE ONE

CHAPTER 7 ....................................................................... 68
DEALING WITH EMPLOYMENT AGENCIES:
THE GOOD, THE BAD, AND THE UGLY

CHAPTER 8 ....................................................................... 78
A WORD ABOUT COLLEGES, SECRETARIAL
SCHOOLS AND OTHER PLACES WHERE YOU CAN
WASTE A LOT OF TIME AND MONEY

**CHAPTER 9**          86
THE HIGHLY SCIENTIFIC CARROLL YAWNOMETER
OF FRIGHTFULLY BORING JOBS

**CHAPTER 10**          94
JOB INTERVIEWS—EVERYBODY'S FAVORITE
ACTIVITY (AFTER ROOT CANAL SURGERY
WITHOUT ANESTHETIC)

**CHAPTER 11**          104
TEN QUESTIONS TO ASK BEFORE YOU TAKE THIS
JOB—FOR RICHER OR FOR POORER

**CHAPTER 12**          114
HOW TO BE A GREAT SECRETARY (WITHOUT BEING
SO GOOD THAT THEY WON'T GIVE YOU A
PROMOTION

**CHAPTER 13**          125
THE SECRETARY'S WHITE-OUT DIET AND EXERCISE
PLAN

**CHAPTER 14**          130
OFFICE AUTOMATION: THE SECRETARY—
AN ENDANGERED SPECIES?

**CHAPTER 15**          137
ADVICE FOR BOSSES ON HOW TO PLEASE YOUR
SECRETARY

**CHAPTER 16**          141
WARNING: SECRETARIAL WORK CAN BE
HAZARDOUS TO YOUR HEALTH

**CHAPTER 17**          166
9 TO 5 AND OTHER SECRETARY LAMENTS AND
WORK DAY SONGS

**CHAPTER 18**          170
OFFICE POLITICS: A SURVIVAL MANUAL FOR
SECRETARIES

**CHAPTER 19**          178
SNAPPY THINGS I WISH I HAD THE NERVE TO SAY
TO MY BOSS

**CHAPTER 20**          182
HITCHING YOUR WAGON TO A STAR: THE EASY
RIDE TO THE TOP

**CHAPTER 21**          185
THE SECRETARY'S HALL OF FAME (...FOR THE
GREAT AND NEAR GREAT)

**CHAPTER 22**                                               **198**
    **30 THINGS YOU CAN DO TO GET YOURSELF**
    **PROMOTED**

**CHAPTER 23**                                               **208**
    **A FINAL WORD FOR WOMEN ONLY**

**APPENDIX A**                                               **217**

**APPENDIX B**                                             **234**

**APPENDIX C**                                             **239**

*ive me an ancient proverb to
introduce a chapter and I will give
you a book that will look like it was
written by an intelligent person.*

*(Ancient Proverb)*

# PREFACE

You don't have to have a Ph.D. in economics to recognize that the current job prospects for secretaries are exceptionally good. With the possible exception of jobs in the computer field, there is no single occupation that will grow as rapidly as this one in the coming decade. Being a secretary offers a person a good paying job with decent benefits and some opportunity for advancement. It also has the unique characteristic of being an occupation that allows one to move anywhere in the country and find a job at a salary commensurate with what that person made at her/his last job.

*Why is it then that becoming a secretary is not considered to be a good career decision?*

## WHAT I WANT TO BE WHEN I GROW UP

When I was growing up during the late fifties and early sixties becoming a secretary was a popular choice for many young women. Women were usually not encouraged to go on to college so that the career choices were more limited than they are today. Still, those of us who chose to become secretaries felt that we had made a smart choice.

The favorable treatment that the media gave to secretaries at the time contributed to our enthusiasm. In television shows like Private Secretary or Perry Mason, the secretary was always the perfect role model — efficient, personable, thorough and honest. The image of the independent-minded woman who was often the brains behind her male boss was one that was constantly being reinforced.

I don't mean to imply that everything was as wonderful in real life as it was on the silver screen. It wasn't. Women in general, and secretaries in particular, were uniformly treated as second-class citizens. No matter how bright she was, or how hard she worked, it was impossible for a woman to be treated equally with her male counterparts. And when it came to wages — there was no parity whatsoever.

## THE WOMEN'S MOVEMENT — FRIEND AND ENEMY

The women's movement of the 1960s and 1970s changed all of that — for better and for worse. Banding together as never before, women struggled against outright oppression and an even more insidious foe — the conditioning that made women believe they were inferior to men. The battles were fought in the schools, in the work places and in the hearts and minds of people everywhere. And women won. And women felt good about winning. And women felt good about themselves.

Gradually attitudes changed and women who sought a place in the corporate board room were no longer considered freaks or lesbians. Business schools and law schools were overwhelmed with the number of female applicants seeking to register. The media started to give a more balanced presentation of the role of women in society. And the courts and legislatures allowed women to truly exert their rights for the first time. It was a wonderful time to be a woman.

## SECRETARY IS A DIRTY WORD

In the fight to win the war, the main battalions of the women's movement trampled some of its own infantry. Housewives and secretaries were the most serious casualties. Neither group has yet to recover. It's not hard to understand why this happened. Housewives and secretaries were the most painfully obvious examples of men's domination of women. At home and in the office men said, "Jump" and the women answered "How high?"

When a spokesperson for the movement sought an example of the oppression of women, she would inevitably point to a sexist husband or a manipulative boss. In doing so she consciously or unconsciously reinforced the notion that housewives or secretaries were not only undesirable vocations — they were outright embarassments to the sisterhood.

I think it's important to remember that, almost without exception, the most well-known leaders of the women's movement were upper-middle class or college-educated or both. They were not women who were secretaries — they were women who *had* secretaries. Their dreams for women were largely upper-middle class, college-educated dreams...women on the Supreme Court, women bank presidents, even a woman in the White House. I don't mean to imply that these goals are any less honorable simply because they were much more attainable for the women who proposed them. Nor do I wish to diminish in any way the personal or overall accomplishments of the leaders of the movement who gave so generously of their time and their souls.

But the legacy of their rhetoric and their tactics in undeniable — women who are secretaries are second-class citizens, (not in the eyes of men because that's always been the case, but in the eyes of their sisters in the women's movement).

## VERWORKED AND UNDERPAID

### I'M A... I'M A... SECRETARY

Titles like "Administrative Assistant," "Girl Friday," or "Executive Aide" have become popular today because women are afraid to acknowledge to other people (...or to themselves) that they are employed as secretaries. This low self-image has also been reinforced by the media. Instead of the strong independent-minded secretary portrayed in the television shows of the fifties and sixties, we now had secretaries with big boobs and little brains (such as the characters played by Carol Burnett and Loni Anderson). Even the comic strips went from career girls like Winnie Winkle to bubble-heads like Miss Buxley. Commercials, too, added to the notion that secretaries were idiots by trying to sell office equipment with the implication that it was so advanced that even a secretary couldn't screw it up.

## OTHERS TO BLAME

The women's movement and the media are only two of the reasons for the deteriorating image of secretaries. There are many others. For example a declining birth rate when coupled with a larger percentage of women going on to college means that the pool of qualified women who might become secretaries has been seriously diminished. Declining educational standards as evidenced by the precipitous drop in SAT scores (and recently reaffirmed by the Presidential task force report on education) indicates that people going into the workforce are not as well prepared as they should be. And then there are secretaries themselves, who by virtue of their poor work habits and appearance are often their own worst enemies.

## TEMPEST IN A TYPEWRITER

It is estimated that there are 20 million secretaries and clerical workers in the United States. That makes office work the single largest job category in this country. Despite their impressive numbers, this group has no power and no prestige. I would like to see that change.

The initial problem that must be addressed is eliminating the ambiguity about what a secretary is versus what she is not. Nearly every position in a corporation has a specific job description — except that of a secretary. A secretary can be someone who makes $35,000 a year with important responsibilities as an assistant to a corporation's chief executive officer or it can be someone who is working at a first job out of high school for a paltry $8,000.

## UNIFORM JOB TITLES FOR SECRETARIES

One solution would be to create a uniform set of job titles (e.g. Executive Secretary, Professional Secretary, Secretary and Junior

Secretary) each of which indicates a range of experience, responsibility and compensation. The problem in trying to create such a structure is that secretarial jobs are currently linked so closely to the status of the person that the secretary works for rather than any normal parameters such as ability or complexity of the job tasks. Accordingly, if an individual has achieved high executive status — so too, will her/his secretary be accorded higher status and greater pay (even if her/his skills and experience are only half as good as another secretary who is working for some lower-level manager). Another problem in trying to establish a uniform system is that many bosses tend to overstate the qualifications of the secretarial position in order to justify their own importance within the organization. Despite these obstacles I believe that it would be possible to create this type of system even if it's only on an industry-by-industry basis.

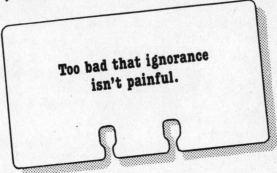

Too bad that ignorance isn't painful.

## RAISES NOT ROSES

In addition to creating titles that permit comparisons among jobs, secretaries must fight for a better salary structure. THERE IS ABSOLUTELY NOTHING THAT CAN IMPROVE THE IMAGE OF SECRETARIES FASTER THAN HIGHER SALARIES. How many times have you heard a boss refer to his secretary by saying, "she knows much more about it than I do" or "when I'm away she runs the office like clockwork"? If that's the case why is the executive making $75,000 and the secretary making $15,000? So the next time that you're rewarded for a job well done with twenty dollars worth of roses — say thank you; then tell your boss what you really want — a significant salary increase. Money is power. Money is status. And money is the place to start if secretaries ever hope to professionalize their jobs in any meaningful way.

## STEVE, COME IN HERE AND TAKE DICTATION!

Another way to improve the prestige of the job (as much as I hate to admit it) is if more men entered the field. During the past decade there has been a dramatic increase in the number of male secretaries. However men still account for less than one percent of all secretarial jobs. I believe that if being a secretary became a socially accepted occupation for men, it would lead to an attitudinal change by men in general (such as we have seen occur in the teaching profession). And you can be sure that male secretaries would never put up with the baloney from male bosses that female secretaries do!

## AND OTHER CHANGES

Another mechanism for change is the possibility that office workers might be organized into a cohesive union. If handled correctly it could mean not only an increase in benefits but also an increase in status as well. There are also lawsuits which will hopefully result in pay equity and improvement of other conditions. But in order for there to be any significant changes the real cataclysm has to occur with the attitudes of women themselves. The women who are secretaries have to come to respect themselves and their jobs (without losing sight of the fact that this position could serve as a stepping-stone to other things). And the women who employ secretaries have to recognize that women who are secretaries, are pursuing a noble occupation which in its own way is no less important than their own.

**I THINK WOMEN WHO HAVE AN ELITIST ATTITUDE TOWARD SECRETARIES ARE WORSE THAN MEN WHO DO.**

**MEN WHO ACT THAT WAY WERE JUST BORN STUPID.**

**BUT WOMEN WHO ACT THAT WAY HAD TO LEARN IT FROM STUPID MEN.**

This book will attempt to clarify what it means to be a great secretary. If it glorifies the role of being a secretary, that's good. If it helps someone to get a higher-paying secretarial job, that's better. And if it shows someone how to use her/his secretarial position as a stepping-stone to a job in management, that's the best of all!

CHAPTER

# 1

# HOW TO FIND A $250,000 A YEAR JOB BY READING THIS BOOK (...AND OTHER RIDICULOUS MYTHS AND LIES PERPETRATED BY HOW-TO-FIND-A-JOB BOOKS)

## HELP WANTED

American society in the eighties seems to be in sad shape. Apparently we need books to tell us how to be nice to each other. Books to teach us how to talk to one another. We need books to tell us how to reduce our thighs and books to tell us how to get those thighs around a potential husband. Can *"How To Handle Your Own Open Heart Surgery"* be far behind? Clearly we are the "How To" generation.

With so many people unemployed or unhappy with their current jobs, it's not surprising that there is a whole bookshelf full of *How To Find the Greatest Job In The Whole World* books. Add this one to the list — maybe.

I've always had great success at getting a good job. With a few exceptions the jobs I've held have been fun, and I've been extremely well paid. A friend of mine who has been stuck in the same miserable job for the past ten years always tells me how lucky I am. I'm firmly convinced that luck has very little to do with it; finding a top job or getting promoted involves knowing what to do, when to do it, and how to do it. That's what this book is all about. But I'd rather start by telling you what it's not about.

This is a "How To" book with some important differences from the other "How To" books in the job field because:

**(1) I WILL NOT STROKE YOU.** I will not tell you what you want to hear just so that you can feel good about yourself. Nor will I tell you nonsense like, "You can be whatever you want to be." If you think that this, or any other book, is going to deliver you from the typing pool to the pool at the Beverly Hills Hotel, save your money.

**(2) I WILL NOT TREAT YOU AS THOUGH YOU HAVE THE SAME INTELLIGENCE QUOTIENT AS THE AVERAGE GERBIL.** Most of the other "How To" job books tell you things like "Be sure to dress neat for interviews" or "Don't have any misspelled (. . .or is that mispelled) words on your resume." I start with the assumption that you didn't permanently check your brains in the eighth-grade coat room and try to concentrate on the things that are not so obvious.

# OVERWORKED AND UNDERPAID

**(3) THIS BOOK IS WRITTEN BY SOMEONE WHO HAS BEEN CONSISTENTLY SUCCESSFUL AT GETTING HIGH-PAYING JOBS.** Everyone loves to read about the woman who invested $500 and made $5 million in the stock market or the man who turned a one-room shack into a real estate empire. If you think you can do it, too, give it a shot. But that's not what this book is about. This book is about home runs — not grand slams. It's about making a lot more money than you make right now, but not retiring when you're 40. It's about the attainable things that the average person can accomplish, enjoy and be proud of — and it's written by someone who did it, not some researcher who has no idea about what it's like to work 9 to 5.

# THE NEW JOB MYTHS

The following is a list of myths that have been created and perpetuated by the recent glut of "How To" job books. Each myth is rated for truth by my special Snow Job Barometer.

## SNOW JOB BAROMETER

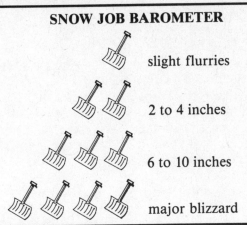

slight flurries

2 to 4 inches

6 to 10 inches

major blizzard

## JOB MYTH NO. 1

**You Can Be Whatever You Want To Be.** Anytime you see that phrase, just ask yourself one question, "If that's true, why would the person who wrote it still be spending her/his time writing 'How To' books?"

## JOB MYTH NO. 2

**You Can Be Successful By Wearing The "Right" Shoes, Carrying The "Right" Briefcase, Etc.** The people who serve up this baloney are obviously trying to justify why they just spent $700 for a pair of shoes that are only worth $80. There's no question that you have to dress for success, but designer clothes and accoutrements are not a necessary part of one's wardrobe. My advice is to take the money that you would have spent on a designer briefcase and go out and buy one or two well-tailored suits.

## JOB MYTH NO. 3

**It's Not The Most Skilled Person Who Gets A Job. It's The Person Who Is Most Skilled At Finding Jobs.** This is only a half-myth because there is some truth to the fact that someone who is adept at locating jobs will have an advantage over someone who isn't. What I find troublesome about this statement is that it fosters the misperception that if you can find jobs other people don't know about, you're likely to get those jobs. This just isn't true in the current job market. Unless an employer is under a tremendous time pressure to fill an opening, that employer is likely to interview several people (or several dozen people) before offering somebody the job. *Finding jobs is only one-fourth of the overall equation — getting offered the job, holding on to the job and getting promoted to a better job is the rest of it.*

## JOB MYTH NO. 4

**You Can Get The Inside Track On A Good Job By Learning How To Anticipate Which Job Fields Will Be The Growth Industries In The Next Ten Years.** I think this was first said by the man who was the leading importer of Nehru jackets during the sixties. Theoretically, you should always take a visionary approach and try to anticipate what things will look like in the future. The problem is that even the so-called experts can't do this very well. Technological and economic conditions vacillate so quickly that yesterday's growth industry can be tomorrow's no industry. And even when you can identify a few of these fields, there are still problems such as these: are you willing to relocate yourself to another part of the country where a new industry is based? Is this the type of business that you're interested in? ( . . . I wouldn't care if you told me that insurance companies will own the world in ten years — and they very well might — working for an insurance company is borrrrrrrrrrrring.)

Never underestimate the power of human stupidity.

## JOB MYTH NO. 5

**Joining A Professional Group Organized Around A Particular Industry Will Help You Get A Job In That Field Or Will Assist You In Obtaining A Promotion.** This is a concept that is sometimes called "networking" and while it's a good long-term career move, it's a lousy way to get a job. Some of these groups have very strict selection procedures which usually mean that the younger members (who could probably benefit most from such an affiliation) are the ones who are least likely to get in. Even after you're admitted, there's really not much going on beyond an occasional luncheon or lecture program. On balance, professional groups are a good thing but not to somebody who needs to find a job in the immediate future.

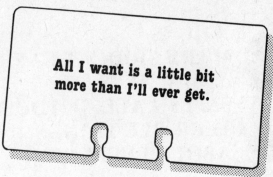

All I want is a little bit more than I'll ever get.

## JOB MYTH NO. 6

**A Well Prepared Résumé Is Your Key To A Great Job.** This is such a popular misconception that I've devoted an entire chapter to it (see Chapter 5).

## JOB MYTH NO. 7

**You Can Invent A Job For Yourself By Presenting Yourself As Someone Who Has The Solutions To A Company's Problems.** This is a typical example of how some well-intentioned job book writer can cause you to waste your valuable time. Think about it — do you really believe you are going to be able to identify and solve the problems of a company that you've never worked for? And don't you think even if you could identify these problems that somebody in the company must be able to see them too (and in all likelihood is already working on them)? Even assuming you were able to identify some genuine problem or need that the company has overlooked — do you honestly think that they're going to hire you to remedy it? Of course not — they'll look for somebody who is already on their staff or somebody who has more experience in the field.

## THE BOTTOM LINE

Don't waste your time on ideas that sound good but have no real practical application.

CHAPTER

# 2

# WHO IS MARY BRIDGET CARROLL AND WHY IS SHE SAYING ALL OF THOSE TERRIBLE THINGS ABOUT EVERYONE?

## BREAKING AWAY

In evaluating anything you do on behalf of your career you should always ask yourself the question, "Is this worth the investment of my time?" In order to make that determination about this book, you need to know something about me. So here goes.

When I was a senior at St. Mary's High School in Greenwich, Connecticut I was hopelessly in love. All I wanted was to graduate, get married and live happily ever after. In those days most parents sent their sons to college and their daughters to secretarial school. My parents offered me a choice — I could go to college or I could go to college. We compromised — I went to junior college. Two years later I had a degree in Occupational Therapy and a strong conviction to postpone the marriage idea for a while. I took a job as a therapist in a private psychiatric hospital. Within a year I knew it wasn't for me and decided to go to New York and look for what I remember calling "a real job."

## THE BIG APPLE TWO-STEP

My opening reviews in the Big Apple were impressive. I had my pick from dozens of job offers — only one minor problem: none of them paid more than $80 a week. I took a job as a receptionist for a textile firm. My "office" was beautifully decorated — fresh flowers twice a week. VIPs called me by my first name. Everything was great — for three weeks. Then I started becoming bored. Real bored! It was then that I made my first upwardly mobile decision — I wanted to become a secretary. But, I had a LARGE problem, two in fact. I couldn't type or take shorthand. I solved the first problem by having all the secretaries in the office agree to give me their extra typing. (...talk about instant popularity!) Within three months I had my degree from the Hunt and Peck School of Typing and shortly afterward I won my first promotion. I was made the secretary to the director of public relations (earning the lofty sum of $85 a week!).

## U 2 cn get a gd jb

I worked at that job for a little over a year. When I was told I couldn't get a raise unless I learned shorthand — I decided to learn shorthand. I followed those "U 2 cn lrn 2 spdrte" signs to a technical school and 3 months later I had my certificate. When the company still refused to give me the raise — I gave them a piece of my mind and my notice.

# VERWORKED AND UNDERPAID

OMEBODY'S ALWAYS SAYING EHIND EVERY SUCCESSFUL 1AN THERE'S A WOMAN.

THEY SHOULD SAY, *NEXT* TO EVERY SUCCESSFUL MAN IS A WOMAN WHO DESERVES HER SHARE OF THAT SUCCESS.

MEET THE SUCCESSFUL WOMAN BEHIND *THIS* SUCCESSFUL WOMAN —BRIDGET CARROLL!

## WORKING FOR THE WO^MAN

I figured with my newly acquired skills I'd take the business world by storm. After dozens of unsuccessful interviews I realized I couldn't even start a drizzle. I had a few jobs but they were all fairly routine with absolutely no possibility for advancement. Then I went to work for a woman who started as a secretary and fought her way up to the number two spot in a public relations firm. Boy, was she tough to work for! The pencils in her desk not only had to be sharpened twice a day, but they all had to be a certain length and placed neatly in her center drawer going in the same direction. And if they weren't just right, or if anything else was not just the way she demanded it to be — watch out! This woman could paralyze you with a single look.

## PAYING YOUR DUES

As much as I disliked her in the beginning, that woman taught me the importance of being a good secretary. I know it sounds trite but if you want to succeed, you have to pay your dues. Chances are you'll have to do a lot of things you don't like, but if you're smart, you'll figure a way to use it to your advantage (or just use it to motivate you to go out and get another job!).

Eventually, my boss recommended me for a junior account executive spot. I was so excited — I couldn't wait to tell everyone I knew about my good fortune. That was a mistake! A few days later I learned that they hired somebody else for the job — somebody who knew about one-tenth as much as I did. When I asked why I wasn't hired, I was told it was because I didn't have a bachelor's degree. I decided that working for this company would prove to be a real dead-end — so I decided to hit the road again.

## MOTIVATION OR STARVATION

I spent the next few months interviewing (I was usually so nervous I couldn't remember my name), working as a babysitter and collecting unemployment. With death from starvation rapidly approaching and my self-esteem at an all-time low, I decided to do something to change my luck. I called everyone I knew and told them that I was looking for a job. I asked friends, previous bosses. I even asked the drycleaning man! Finally, a woman I went to college with called to tell me about an opening at a midtown law firm. Even though I didn't think my skills would be strong enough to get the job I decided to give it a shot.

## AN UNUSUAL INTERVIEW

I arrived in my usual state of high anxiety. To make matters worse, the lawyer was an hour and a half late. Finally he came dashing in, said he had to meet his mother uptown, and asked me if I would agree to be interviewed in a cab on the way there (. . . in my financial state, I would have agreed to the interview on the roof of the cab!). As it turned out, I wound up being interviewed by both the lawyer and his mother. It was all so unorthodox and happened so quickly that I forgot to be nervous. As a result I passed inspection and was offered the job on the spot.

## MY FIRST BIG BREAK

Being a legal secretary can be a pretty boring job, but this one wasn't. In addition to being a lawyer, my boss (...as lawyers would say, "Hereinafter referred to as Ed") had recently been elected to the New York State Assembly. This meant that there would be a great deal of constituent and legislative work that had to be done. It also meant that I would have to make a six-hour car trip to the State Capital in Albany and back — twice a week. Ed assured me that if I was willing to put in the time and learn the job, he would give me all the responsibility I wanted. That was just the opportunity I had been looking for.

During the next four years I worked on bills dealing with important issues like capital punishment and gun control. I also handled the normal secretarial functions of running the office. As I became more experienced I found Ed was willing to listen to my comments and ideas. Eventually he trusted me enough to let me do a certain number of jobs without waiting for his approval. By the time Ed decided to retire from the legislature I felt I knew more about politics than people with a Ph.D. in Political Science. (They should have given me an L.B.E. degree for knowing a Little Bit of Everything.)

I thought going back to being a full-time secretary would be a real disappointment, but it wasn't. Ed had a number of interesting cases and clients (including tennis ace Jimmy Connors). During this period I traveled to some great places and met a number of celebrities. And, I was well paid.

## WHAT I WANT TO BE WHEN I GROW UP — CHAP. 2

As much as I was enjoying the job, I realized it was time for a new challenge — preferably a non-secretarial position. With the help of contacts I had made during my tenure with Ed, I was able to find a spot rather easily. I took a junior management position with a small cosmetic company. I stayed at that job for a year and, although I learned a lot, ultimately I decided I wasn't the right type for a career in the cosmetic field. So, I decided to try something else.

## ONE STEP SIDEWAYS...

By this point, I had no question about my employability. I had the experience and I had the self-confidence to back it up. Within a few weeks I had my pick of several jobs. Believe it or not, I chose to become a secretary again. As far as I was concerned this wasn't a step backward, it was merely a stepping-stone to a spot I really wanted. The job was administrative assistant to the chairman of one of the largest financial institutions in the United States. How much did I know about the financial world? ABSOLUTELY NOTHING. But I had enough confidence in myself to believe that eventually I would find out whatever I needed to know in order to succeed. And I did.

### ...TWO STEPS AHEAD

The more I learned about the world of Wall Street, the more fascinated I became with the role of a stockbroker. Although my boss discouraged me, I was just stubborn enough to want to give it a try. So at 35 years old, I went back to school (...this was the same person who at 20 said "Thank God I don't ever have to study again!"). Several months later I took my licensing test and, after a couple of stabs at it, passed.

### MINOR COMPLICATIONS

Now I was ready to set up shop as a stockbroker. There was only one minor complication — I had no clients. My list started and ended with my parents. Thank goodness for parents. And, thank goodness for my secretarial training. As a result of dealing with different people and situations for so many years, I found that I had no problem calling perfect strangers to solicit their business. Being a secretary also gave me an understanding of the kind of efficiency and personal attention clients expect from people who are in the personal service business.

### BECOMING ONE OF "THEM"

My first year as a stockbroker, I made ten thousand dollars more than I had in my best year as a secretary. In my second year as a stockbroker, I will probably make three to four times more. I have to be honest, I never thought I'd ever make this kind of money. And the best part of all is — I've only just begun!

### HOW I CAME TO WRITE THIS BOOK

One day I was practicing my Tai Chi after chanting a mantra (and before starting my macrobiotic dinner) when I got a call from my guru. He told me that my Pluto was in the sixth house and my biorhythms were perfect for starting this book. Right now, if danger lights aren't flashing on and off in your head and you aren't thinking "I can't believe that I just blew my hard-earned dough on a book written by some granola flake," then you deserve to stay in a low-paying job.

I wrote this book because I was tired of what I called the EST-Rolfing-TM-Hare Krishna approach to job improvement. I'm talking about:

people who encourage you to carry a notebook around with you at all times so that you can faithfully record every aspect of your daily routine. ( . . . I have a tough enough time remembering to carry my housekeys.)

people who tell you things like, "Think of life as one big strong oak tree with the branches being the variety of life's experiences." ( . . . Makes you want to climb away, doesn't it?)

people who urge you to continually ask yourself questions like, "Where are you? And where are you going in the next ten years? How are you going to get there?" ( . . . People who know where they're going to be ten years from now have nothing in common with me. I'm concerned with more mundane things like, "I hope to God my rent check doesn't bounce.")

people who tell you to write out a classified ad that constitutes your ideal job — then go out and find the job that incorporates all of those characteristics. ( . . . I tried it and found the only job that had all the money, status, clothes and lack of responsibility I wanted was being Robert Redford's wife, and that spot was already taken.)

## YOU CAN DO ANYTHING. BALONEY!

I don't believe that authors like those referred to above are necessarily fast-buck artists or charlatans. In most cases I think they are well-intentioned people who are simply trying to apply some of the "you can do anything" mentality from the consciousness-raising movement to the job field. The trouble is people like us, with ordinary jobs and/or kids and/or charge account balances and/or mortgages and/or degrees from ordinary schools and colleges and/or 15 other ordinary realities simply do not have the time to waste on anything but the nuts and bolts of getting a good job.

## A REALISTIC APPROACH

This is not to say that many of those books can't be helpful. They can. And this is not to say that many of my strategies for job success don't overlap with many of the strategies of the guru types. They do. What's different about my approach is that it's entirely realistic and it doesn't assume there has to be a radical transformation of your personality in order to get a great job.

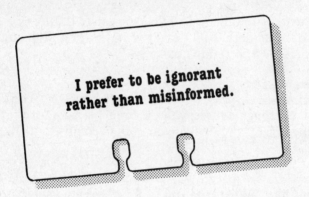

I prefer to be ignorant rather than misinformed.

## THE ART OF SELF-CONFIDENCE

I believe I have been successful primarily because I possess a tremendous amount of self-confidence. But I didn't start out that way — and I don't expect you to be that way either...in the beginning. Self-confidence is an acquired art. People who think they have it, without paying some dues to get it, are usually confusing aggressiveness with self-confidence. In this book I'm giving you many strategies for dealing with people and situations in a job setting. Even if you can only use a few of them at first, you're bound to increase your job importance (and as a result, your own self-confidence). As your faith in yourself continues to build, you'll be able to take on increasingly more demanding challenges.

**You'll know you have completely realized the
level of self-confidence you should have when
you look around one day and it suddenly occurs
to you that there isn't anyone in your office
(including the people pulling down six figures)
who's doing something you couldn't do with a
minimal amount of training and experience.**

## HOW SECRETARIES RATE
## THEIR WORK AND THEIR JOBS

How important are the following to your feelings about work?

|  | Very Important 1981 1972 | Moderately Important 1981 1972 | Not Important 1981 1972 |
|---|---|---|---|
| a) Freedom to organize your own work | 91% 83% | 9% 15% | 0% 6% |
| b) Opportunity to learn new skills | 86% 73% | 14% 23% | 0% 2% |
| c) Opportunity to take increased responsibility | 81% 77% | 18% 20% | 1% 1% |
| d) Opportunity for promotion | 58% 31% | 25% 38% | 17% 30% |

How would you rate your current job on the following points?

|  | Good '81 '72 | Fair '81 '72 | Poor '81 '72 | Not Sure '81 '72 |
|---|---|---|---|---|
| a) Freedom to organize your own work | 86% 87% | 12% 9% | 1% 1% | 0% 3% |
| b) Opportunity to learn new skills | 47% 40% | 35% 40% | 17% 16% | 1% 4% |
| c) Opportunity to take increased responsibility | 47% 50% | 36% 33% | 16% 12% | 1% 5% |
| d) Opportunity for promotion | 18% 16% | 28% 21% | 45% 39% | 8% 14% |

Source: Special Report: Secretaries Tell What They Think, What They Want (1981). Reprinted with permission and copyrighted by The Research Institute of America, Inc.

In this book I am giving you a number of strategies that have worked for me and other successful people I know. It's not a program you must adhere to each day like a diet; but like any good diet, there's nothing that I, or anybody else, can say that will make a difference unless you are committed to making it work.

As you read the rest of this book just keep in mind the words of the famous philosopher Phillystein who once told his followers: *"The Meek Shall Inherit The Left-Overs."*

CHAPTER

# 3

# ONE HUNDRED
# YEARS OF
# SECRETARIES:
# A
# PICTORIAL
# ESSAY

**One of the earliest photographs of a secretary.**

# 1880-1910

Miss Remington 1905.

Early liberationists.

Nasty bosses are not a recent phenomena.

The earliest recorded incident of "Office hanky panky."

RY THIS ON THE TYPEWRITER.

Early 1900s humor.

Daughter of Sholes, the inventor of the typewriter.

Well at least we don't have to wear hats anymore.

An office affair.

# 1920-1940

Office style — 1920s.

Not much has changed in 60 years!

**Maybe computers won't be so bad after all.**

**Secretaries doing their part for the war effort.**

"Office Girls" by Isaac Soyer.

# 1950-1980

*"Could I get up and stretch? It's been a long letter"*

A typical example of jokes about secretaries in mens' magazines.

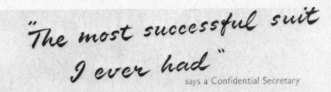

# "The most successful suit I ever had"

says a Confidential Secretary

*It looks right, wears right and makes me feel well dressed and quietly sure of myself. It was made from five yards of 'Moygashel' Harrogate. Only 7/8d. a yard, yet it drapes beautifully, resists creasing and comes up like new each time I wash it.*

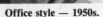

**Office style — 1950s.**

**"Since you have a free hand, Miss Carroll would you mind....**

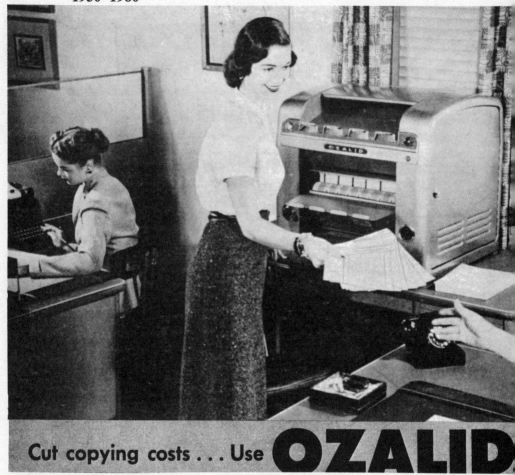

Cut copying costs . . . Use OZALID

A 1950s advertisement.

Filing — the bane of every secretary's existence.

**Miss Wrong.**                    **Miss Right.**

**More office humor — men's style.**

## ES GIBT EIN CODEWORT ZUM ÖFFNEN VON TRESOREI LIEBE.

Es fängt an, wie es immer anfängt:
Man lernt sich kennen. Faßt Zuneigung und Vertra
Geht aus. Und verliebt sich. Gern erzählt man
aus seinem Leben. Intimes. Privates. Und vom Be
Kleine Bitten werden erfüllt. Es werden immer
größere. Aus Liebe. Aber am Ende war
es bloß: Landesverrat.
    Denn manche Liebe ist geplant.
In Ostberlin. Und der Partner ist
längst verheiratet. Mit dem dortigen
Staatssicherheitsdienst.
    Denken Sie bitte daran.

This is a poster warning West German secretaries that the man courting them could be an East German secret agent.

Office style — late 1960s, early 1970s.

I guess we haven't really come such a long way baby.

The secretary of the 1980s.

CHAPTER

# 20 THINGS (GIVE OR TAKE A FEW) YOU CAN DO TO GET YOUR FOOT OUT OF YOUR MOUTH AND INTO THE DOOR OF A GREAT JOB

## LIGHTING YOUR FIRE

Getting a job is no problem, but getting a *great* job can be a tremendous problem. You might think that if someone is good at what she/he does, they would have no problem getting another job. But that's not always the case. There's no correlation between being good at performing a job and being good at getting a job. I know many people who are good at one but not the other.

One encouraging thing is that great jobs do tend to beget other great jobs. This happens because employers will generally assume that most people will function well on the level of their last position — or higher. It also happens because an employee's level of self-confidence tends to increase as she/he progresses to jobs with greater responsibilities. So the real key is this: GETTING YOUR FOOT IN THE DOOR FOR THAT FIRST GREAT JOB.

This entire book is aimed at helping you get off your buns and get that job. Here are a few specific suggestions:

**(1) QUIT YOUR PRESENT JOB:** If you are in a dead-end job with no possibility for advancement the best thing you can do for your career is to quit. It's a rather drastic step to take but I think that most of us need to do something truly significant in order to break the trap of lethargy or security that keeps us confined to jobs we hate. REMEMBER: PEOPLE WHO HAVE SOMETHING TO FALL BACK ON USUALLY FALL BACK ON IT.

**(2) TAKE A JOB (ANY JOB) WHILE YOU'RE LOOKING FOR THE JOB OF YOUR DREAMS:** Needing a job is great motivation for finding a job, but that doesn't mean you have to be unemployed. In fact, being unemployed can prove to be a real negative since many employers are skeptical about hiring somebody who is out of work. (They're thinking to themselves, "If this person is so good how come she/he is unemployed?") The best solution is to take an interim job which you can always explain by saying, "I needed the money" or "I'm just helping out my sister-in-law."

**(3) CONTACT YOUR FRIENDS AND TELL THEM THAT YOU ARE LOOKING FOR A JOB:** Even companies that promote from within must hire a certain percentage of new people each year. Most of these new jobs will be filled by the friends of the current employees. So call everyone you know and get the word out that you're looking for a job. Start with your friends who have the most clout first, but get the word out to everybody. (You will be surprised to find that some very unlikely people become the source of some very promising job leads.)

**(4) MAKE YOUR COVER LETTERS SPECIAL:** Whenever you respond to an ad or make an inquiry about a job, come up with a way to distinguish your letter from the mailbag of other letters an employer is likely to receive on the subject. Start with a strong opening paragraph, then follow it with a brief statement of why you are qualified. The best letters are the ones that simply say, "you're looking for someone with such and such experience; I've got it."

**(5) ALWAYS TRY TO ARRANGE A PERSONAL MEETING:** Most people can sell themselves better in person than they can in a five-minute phone conversation or a one-page resume. Therefore, you should always push for a personal meeting. Just say, "It will only take ten minutes. I guarantee it won't prove to be a waste of your time."

**(6) DON'T JUST THINK OF PEOPLE WHO MIGHT HIRE YOU — THINK OF PEOPLE WHO KNOW PEOPLE WHO MIGHT HIRE YOU:** In any given job field, there are a number of important people who may not hire people themselves but who may be in a position to influence others who do. Editors of trade publications, officers of professional associations and union officials are just some who fall into this category. Even if you don't get a job lead out of it, you will have learned more about the field, expanded your contacts and given yourself the opportunity to drop an important name during some future job interview.

**(7) DON'T BE AFRAID TO BE A LITTLE DIFFERENT:** I bet you know at least two couples where one partner is fairly conservative and the other is fairly wacky. In all likelihood they were drawn together because each has personality traits the other lacks. Relationships among working people are not dissimilar. Therefore when you consider how straight-laced most businessmen are — being different could actually be a plus. (Here's a good rule of thumb to use when trying to decide how different you can be. *Dizzy is bad; flaky is good. Lucy Ricardo is bad; Annie Hall is good.)*

**(8) SEND LETTERS TO PEOPLE AT COMPANIES YOU'VE TARGETED WHO WENT TO THE SAME HIGH SCHOOL OR COLLEGE THAT YOU DID:** One of the best (and most underutilized) job aids is the alumni directory. Independent companies now make deals with schools to periodically publish a directory of everyone who graduated from a particular school together with their home addresses, company affiliations and titles. Even if the person you contact is in a completely different part of the company from where you hope to be, send a letter and ask for an introduction to someone in the right department.

> **NEVER TELL YOUR FAMILY OR EVEN YOUR FRIENDS THAT YOU'RE UP FOR A JOB UNTIL YOU GET IT. THAT WAY, YOU'LL ELIMINATE A WHOLE LOT OF UNNECESSARY PRESSURE.**

**(9) IF YOU WANT TO TALK TO A PROSPECTIVE EMPLOYER, CALL HER/HIM AFTER 5 O'CLOCK:** Many secretaries leave at 5; most executives don't. If you do get the secretary on the phone, say that you're calling about something personal. Don't lie but try to avoid telling her/him that you're calling about a job.

**(10) FIX A REALISTIC TIMETABLE BY WHICH YOU HOPE TO ATTAIN CERTAIN GOALS:** One thing that happens to all of us is that we promise ourselves we're going to change jobs but we never do. Occasionally we might take a stab at doing something about it, but inevitably we find that years have passed and we're still in the same place marking time. Fixing a schedule will create a certain amount of pressure on us to do something about completing the goals we've outlined for ourselves. (REMEMBER — NOTHING MOTIVATES BETTER THAN GUILT.)

(11) **THINK UNTRADITIONALLY:** I know a woman who wanted to go into business for herself but as we Irish like to say, "She hadn't a pot to pee in." Then she hit upon a great idea. She wrote to a number of small accounting firms asking if they represented anyone interested in selling their business to someone who would pay them the purchase price out of each year's earnings over a certain period of time. It worked so well that she had three different business opportunities to choose from. Today the woman is in the apparel business and can afford 14 karat gold bathroom commodes.

(12) **NEVER TURN DOWN AN INTERVIEW:** You just may learn something at one interview that will enhance your chances of getting a job somewhere else.

# VERWORKED AND UNDERPAID

(13) **LOOK AT WHAT PEOPLE ARE DOING IN OTHER PARTS OF THE COUNTRY (OR EVEN OTHER PARTS OF YOUR OWN STATE) AND SEE IF YOU CAN APPLY IT LOCALLY TO YOUR OWN ADVANTAGE:** A few years ago a friend saw a television news report about a women in another state who had convinced her company to provide daycare facilities at her plant as a way to attract working mothers and reduce absenteeism. My friend thought it was a great idea so she teamed up with another woman (who had experience in the daycare field)

and made a proposal to several different companies. One of the companies liked the idea and contributed the space and the money to get them started.

**(14) ASK A FRIEND WHO OWNS HER/HIS BUSINESS TO LET YOU LEARN THE BUSINESS:** One way around the proverbial Catch 22 of business: *you can't get a job without experience and you can't get experience without a job* is to find a friend or relative who is willing to let you work in her/his company. If the business is small enough you will be able to give yourself any title you choose (Director of Advertising, Vice President for Sales and Marketing, etc.) — and this will sound great when you write your next resume.

**(15) LEARN TO OPERATE OFFICE EQUIPMENT:** Within a few years virtually every office staff person is going to have to learn how to use a basic computer. Since you're going to have to do it sooner or later, you might as well resign yourself to the fact and do it now. Secretaries who can operate word processors, telex machines and the like usually have a much easier time finding a job (and often make $2,000 to $3,000 more per year than jobs that don't require these skills).

**(16) USE NEPOTISM:** Giving a member of one's family an advantage in hirings and promotions is a fact of life in the business world. I know a lot of people who resent the fact that the boss' son or daughter is given a position that other, more qualified people deserve. It doesn't bother me. I figure that nepotism has been around for a long time and always will be. *Instead of wasting time worrying about other people who got their jobs through nepotism, devote your energies to getting yourself a position with which you will have the power to give jobs to your own family.*

**(17), (18), (19), (20)** Ever since I started writing this book, I've been wondering how other writers are able to get their list of suggestions or tips to always come out to an even number like 20. I now realize that either they're piling on the baloney or they're lucky. Of course, if it makes you feel as though you're getting your money's worth, I could add some inane heading like, "Add your four favorite reasons here."

## ...AND THINGS NOT TO DO

**(1) DON'T PUT AN AD IN THE NEWSPAPER TELLING COMPANIES HOW WONDERFUL YOU ARE:** The only people you'll hear from are employment agencies.

**(2) DON'T SEND OUT COVER LETTERS ON THE STATIONARY OF YOUR PRESENT EMPLOYER:** Ordinarily, I would assume that's pretty obvious, except I've seen so many people do it.

**(3) DON'T WASTE A LOT OF TIME WITH COLLEGE OR BUSINESS SCHOOL PLACEMENT OFFICES:** Pay them a visit, but don't waste too much time with them. They're usually pretty ineffective for anyone except the most recent graduates.

**SPORTS**

**LEARN TO PLAY THE "RIGHT" SPORTS**

**"RIGHT" SPORTS**

ROWING   RACQUET-BALL   MARATHON RUNNING   GOLF

**"WRONG" SPORTS**

HUNTING   ARM WRESTLING   HANDBALL   DRAG RACING

**(4) DON'T STUMBLE IF YOU'RE ASKED WHY YOU WERE FIRED FROM YOUR LAST JOB:** Have a short, direct, non-defensive answer prepared well in advance.

**(5) DON'T TAKE ON A JOB UNLESS YOU ARE QUALIFIED AND CAPABLE OF DOING IT WELL:** It's better to pass up a good job that you just can't handle than to take it on and screw it up.

**(6) DON'T TAKE A JOB IN A SECRETARIAL POOL:** Unless you're absolutely desperate, avoid secretarial pools at all costs. These jobs are usually the worst positions in any company (which probably accounts for the fact that the turnover is three times greater than secretaries who work for a single boss). If you find yourself in a secretarial pool — start to back stroke as fast as you can!

**(7) DON'T HITCH YOUR WAGON TO SOMEBODY WHO'S GOING NOWHERE:** One very good way to get ahead is to become affiliated with somebody whose career is on the rise (see Chapter 20). One good way to get fired or languish in the same boring job forever is to become too closely identified with somebody who is going nowhere.

**ADD YOUR OWN FAVORITE "THINGS NOT TO DO" HERE:**

(8) _____

(9) _____

(10)_____

## HOW SECRETARIES RATE THEIR STATUS COMPARED TO OTHER JOBS

|  | More respected | Less respected | About same | Not sure | No answer |
|---|---|---|---|---|---|
| Salesmen | 21% | 39% | 28% | 9% | 3% |
| Supervisors | 8 | 63 | 23 | 4 | 2 |
| Engineers | 6 | 69 | 12 | 10 | 3 |
| Stenographers | 64 | 5 | 24 | 4 | 3 |
| Office Managers | 9 | 57 | 26 | 5 | 3 |
| Clerks | 73 | 6 | 14 | 4 | 3 |
| Correspondents | 29 | 18 | 25 | 23 | 5 |
| Buyers | 11 | 44 | 24 | 17 | 4 |

Source: Report entitled "What Every Executive Should Know About His Secretary". Reprinted with permission and copyrighted by The Research Institute of America, Inc.

**CHAPTER**

# 5

## THE RÉSUMÉ (A BRIEF COURSE IN CREATIVE WRITING)

### ONLY WASPESE SPOKEN HERE

About ten years ago I interviewed for a job with a Wall Street law firm. It was one of those old mahogany firms with a name like Gold, Frankensense and Murr. I really didn't want the job (law firms are bor-r-ring; see Carroll Yawnometer Chapter 9), but the money was extraordinary (as was the level of my poverty at the time). The interview was conducted by a guy who was so old that he looked like he had passed away several years before. Not surprisingly, the guy was Brooks Brothers clear down to his tassel loafers and spoke only Waspese, which requires the uncanny ability to be able to enunciate perfectly through tightly clenched teeth.

### YOUR CURRICULUM VITAE IS SHOWING

The old codger wasted no time in sorting out the Brooklyns from the Brahmins by asking me if I had my "curriculum vitae." From the blank expression on my face, he knew he would have to repeat what he said and did so as though he were speaking to a non-English speaking foreigner. "Cur•ric•u•lum vi•tae," he said as he carefully pronounced every single syllable. Thinking that it must have something to do with school (...curriculum — school...get the connection?) I quickly answered, "I didn't know I was supposed to bring a school transcript."

## WHERE TO FILE YOUR RÉSUMÉ

From old chalk-stripes' expression of frustration, I figured I could safely rule out school transcript as a possible answer. "Your c.v., young lady, didn't you bring your c.v.?", inquired the old geezer, obviously enjoying his brief moment of superiority. Clearly, if I didn't know what a curriculum vitae was, calling it by its initials wasn't going to help me any. What I should have told him was, "You can have my c.v. provided you s.i.i.y.e.y.o.s. (stick it in your ear, you old schlub). Unfortunately, like most people, I dream up my best retorts only after the fact.

Finally, old white bread decided to give me a break, "your résumé — don't you have a résumé?" In fact, I did, but by that time it was plain that he had no intention of offering this job to someone who didn't speak Latin, and I had no intention of working for a firm that would employ an old snoot like this guy.

## NO PART OF THE JOB HUNTING PROCESS IS MORE OVERRATED THAN THE PREPARATION OF A RÉSUMÉ.

## THE RÉSUMÉ GURUS

If you can't find a job and you're absolutely desperate for work, I would recommend that you open a résumé writing service. It requires no license, no formal education, nothing but what we Irish like to call the gift of the blarney. Better yet, write a book on how to prepare a résumé — there's only a few dozen of those around.

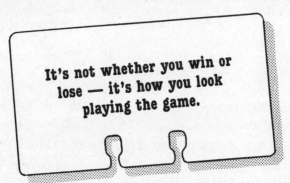

It's not whether you win or lose — it's how you look playing the game.

In the 1980s a well-prepared resume is no longer an exception — it's a given. Anyone from a high school guidance teacher to an employment agency counselor can show you how to do it — and they won't charge you a nickel for the privilege. Don't spend a lot of time and energy trying to write the perfect résumé — just write a tight, straight-forward statement of your career goals and experiences. It's important to remember that most employers are not complete dolts; they know when an applicant is trying to make nothing seem like something. If you're just starting out and have very little experience, you can't rely on your résumé to get a job — or even an interview. You have to get out and hustle. You have to make yourself stand out from the crowd (this book will give you some suggestions about how to accomplish that).

## ERWORKED AND UNDERPAID

T SEND US
JR RESUME.

SURE--BUT IF YOU'LL GIVE ME AS MUCH TIME AS IT TAKES TO READ IT, I'LL SHOW YOU I'M THE RIGHT PERSON FOR THE JOB.

YOU'VE GOT SPUNK-- I LIKE THAT. BE HERE TOMORROW AT TEN.

### BRIDGET'S RULES OF RÉSUMÉ WRITING

Here are 14 rules for writing a competent résumé (plus the Bridget Carroll Magic Word List which will automatically transform even the most unremarkable c.v. to a state of the art résumé):

**RÉSUMÉ RULE NO. 1** The word résumé has two accents — one over each e. Therefore it's spelled résumé.

**RÉSUMÉ RULE NO. 2** The single most important function that a résumé serves is to get you an interview — as long as it accomplishes that, it's a good résumé.

**RÉSUMÉ RULE NO. 3** Nobody is interested in your memoirs — keep it brief. A one-page résumé is plenty until you have enough genuine experience to expand to two pages.

**RÉSUMÉ RULE NO. 4** Determine what your job objective is first; — then work backward to be sure that your résumé justifies the fact that you deserve to get that job.

**RÉSUMÉ RULE NO. 5** Give prominence to your most marketable skills, but don't exaggerate — too much. (It's not hard to figure out that you alone were not responsible for doubling Chrysler's profits last year, especially since your last name isn't Iacocca and you were only an assistant file clerk at the time.)

**RÉSUMÉ RULE NO. 6** Don't be afraid to include some personal information. You'd be amazed at how many job interviews start off with, "So I see that you and your father were ranked 5th in the state as a father-daughter doubles team . . ." — If your prospective employer then goes on to tell you that, "My daughter and I used to be ranked — but that was years ago" — increase your asking price by 40%.

**RÉSUMÉ RULE NO. 7** Don't send a "flower-child, consciousness raising, I've-gotta-be-me" type résumé. You know the type: it inevitably begins with some dumb lead sentence like, "Who is Goldie Goldhair and why is she applying for this job?" Most employers' lead sentence will be "Who cares?"

**RÉSUMÉ RULE NO. 8** Don't underestimate yourself. Take some time to carefully review your work performance during the past few years. Have you ever been responsible for saving the company money? Did you help to identify a situation that people now recognize to be a problem? Did you do anything to change the nature of your job? Did you make it more efficient? By asking yourself some probing questions — you might discover that you accomplished more than you initially thought you did.

**RÉSUMÉ RULE NO. 9** Concentrate on what the résumé says, not what type of format you should use. Some people tell you to use a chronological approach (most recent business experience first, then go backward from there). Others say use a functional approach (which means categorizing your experience into specific skill categories). Still others say use a combination of the two. I say use whatever works — whatever works for you and whatever works for the particular job you're applying for.

**RÉSUMÉ RULE NO. 10** If you list your experience chronologically on your résumé, make sure that each job shows that you were given more responsibility than the previous one.

**RÉSUMÉ RULE NO. 11** Don't assume that the same résumé will work for every job you apply for. You will improve your odds of being offered a job if you attempt to tailor your résumé to each position that you apply for. In short, tell 'em what they want to hear!

**RÉSUMÉ RULE NO. 12** Don't send a prospective employer a photograph — even if you look like Bo Derek's twin sister or Tom Selleck's clone.

**RÉSUMÉ RULE NO. 13** Anything that you've ever done of any consequence can probably be translated into some sort of work experience. Don't assume that because you've been raising a family for the past ten years, you have no job qualifications. Examine things that you've done during this time and think of how they may have some application to skills required in the work world. If for example you have been a volunteer coordinator for the local political party or a fund raiser for the local hospital, you probably have perfected several different skills that would be of interest to prospective employers.

**RÉSUMÉ RULE NO. 14** If you can get a great letter of recommendation from someone with some stature in the same field as the job you're applying for — send it along. The salient adjectives here are "great" ( — if the letter is only good, don't send it!) and "same" ( — if the letter isn't written by someone in the same field or someone fairly prominent who has worked with you personally, then don't waste your time.)

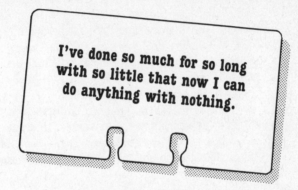

I've done so much for so long with so little that now I can do anything with nothing.

## THE CREATIVE WRITING APPROACH
## TO RÉSUMÉ PREPARATION

I know a lot of people who started off in their careers by lying about their credentials. I think it's a bad idea. Especially since you don't have to. If you've been working for awhile you've probably acquired more experience than you've given yourself credit for — particularly if you're a secretary. Let's say that you've been the secretary at a small magazine. I'll bet you've acquired knowledge in areas as diverse as circulation, editorial, production and account management. Now all you have to do is to learn to present these accomplishments in the most favorable light.

Advertising copywriters make a living out of making the mundane seem sublime. They can take a can of dog food that looks and smells as bad as any other can of dog food and make you believe that it's filet mignon. Let's say that for the past two years you have been a secretary for a small company that makes industrial films. As far as you're concerned your job has been a fairly routine

9 to 5 secretarial position. Consequently the reference to this experience on your résumé might read like this:

10/82
to
Present
    BIMBO COMMUNICATIONS, INC., New York City.
Secretary for this company which makes industrial films.

But with a little gift of the blarney the exact same experience might look like this:

10/82
to
Present
    BIMBO COMMUNICATIONS, INC., New York City.
Secretary to the Vice-President of Marketing (...*alright, so the company only has three principals and each of them handles a dozen different jobs: pick out one that sounds prestigious and include it)* at this fast-growing industrial motion picture film and audio visual production company (...*look through the company's own literature and find out how they describe themselves)* whose clients include General Electric and Ford (...*who cares that the GE film was made six years ago or that the Ford project was a slide show for some minor sales promotion in Muscatine, Iowa)*. In addition to my responsibilities as secretary I also served as office manager (...*so did the other two secretaries — but so what?)*. My overall responsibilities included the preparation and execution of the following:

— purchase orders
— secretarial functions
— invoices
— client and phone contact
— union contracts
— talent coordination
— composed own correspondence

— travel arrangements
— office management
— coordination of free-lance and professional personnel
— equipment and production coordination
— research

So without lying you have shown yourself to be someone who is extremely capable and ready to handle the challenge of a managerial-type position.

# THE BRIDGET CARROLL MAGIC
## WORD LIST FOR RÉSUMÉS

### NOUNS

| | | |
|---|---|---|
| Accomplishment | Determination | Ingenuity |
| Achievement | Development | Initiative |
| Advancement | Direction | Input |
| Ambition | Documentation | Insight |
| Analysis | Drive | Instruction |
| Appearance | Duty | Intelligence |
| Approach | Education | Job |
| Aptitude | Endurance | Judgment |
| Assessment | Energy | Knowledge |
| Attitude | Evaluation | Leadership |
| Award | Executive | Level |
| Candor | Expansion | Loyalty |
| Capability | Experience | Management |
| Capacity | Facts | Manner |
| Challenge | Flexibility | Maturity |
| Common | Forecast | Method |
| Communication | Foresight | Motivation |
| Conference | Framework | Negotiations |
| Control | Function | Objective |
| Cooperation | Goal | Organization |
| Courage | Growth | Panache |
| Creativity | Honesty | Patience |
| Data | Ideas | Performance |
| Dedication | Imagination | Perserverance |
| Demeanor | Implementation | Personality |
| Designation | Information | Pizazz |

**THE BRIDGET CARROLL MAGIC
WORD LIST FOR RÉSUMÉS**

## NOUNS (CONT'D)

| | | |
|---|---|---|
| Policy | Reliability | Specifications |
| Position | Report | Stability |
| Presentation | Requirements | Standards |
| Pride | Research | Strategy |
| Priorities | Resourcefulness | Supervision |
| Procedures | Responsibility | Survey |
| Production | Review | System |
| Proficient | Reward | Tact |
| Profits | Satisfaction | Talent |
| Programs | Savvy | Title |
| Projects | Self-assurance | Training |
| Promotion | Self-confidence | Versatility |
| Purpose | Self-reliance | Vision |
| Qualification | Sense of humor | Vitality |
| Recommendation | Skills | Work flow |
| Records | Solution | Writing |

### THE BRIDGET CARROLL MAGIC
### WORD LIST FOR RÉSUMÉS

**WORDS AND PHRASES**

| | |
|---|---|
| Attended to details | Office flow procedures |
| Bottom line | Open-minded |
| Complete knowledge of | People-oriented |
| Courage of my convictions | Points of view |
| Course of action | Pride in performance |
| Decision maker | Provided feedback |
| Detail-oriented | Qualified by |
| Downside risks | Records management systems |
| Empirical evidence | Reduced costs |
| Excel under pressure | Self-starter |
| Follow through | Supporting data |
| Full charge | Take-charge person |
| Give and take | Team work |
| Goal-oriented | Thinking on my feet |
| Growth potential | Was responsible for |
| Managerial skills | Winner's attitude |
| Manual skills | Work flow |
| Meets deadlines easily | Work without supervision |

### THE BRIDGET CARROLL MAGIC
### WORD LIST FOR RÉSUMÉS

## VERBS

| | | |
|---|---|---|
| Accomplished | Developed | Increased |
| Achieved | Devised | Influenced |
| Advanced | Directed | Inspired |
| Analyzed | Diversified | Instituted |
| Annotated | Drafted | Instructed |
| Applied | Edited | Interpreted |
| Arranged | Educated | Introduced |
| Assisted | Encouraged | Learned |
| Attained | Enhanced | Led |
| Authorized | Established | Maintained |
| Budgeted | Evaluated | Managed |
| Chaired | Exceeded | Marketed |
| Communicated | Exercised | Monitored |
| Compiled | Expanded | Motivated |
| Composed | Expedited | Negotiated |
| Computed | Experienced | Obtained |
| Conceived | Followed | Ordered |
| Conducted | Forecasted | Organized |
| Controlled | Gathered | Originated |
| Coordinated | Guided | Participated |
| Counseled | Handled | Performed |
| Cut | Helped | Perservered |
| Defined | Hired | Persisted |
| Delegated | Initiated | Persuaded |
| Designed | Implemented | Prioritized |
| Determined | Improved | Produced |

**THE BRIDGET CARROLL MAGIC
WORD LIST FOR RÉSUMÉS**

## VERBS (CONT'D)

| | | |
|---|---|---|
| Programmed | Scheduled | Synthesized |
| Promoted | Screened | Systematized |
| Purchased | Selected | Targeted |
| Ran | Set-up | Taught |
| Recommended | Sold | Trained |
| Reduced | Started | Transcribed |
| Reported | Summarized | Understood |
| Represented | Supervised | Updated |
| Researched | Surpassed | Won |
| Reviewed | Surveyed | Wrote |

# THE BRIDGET CARROLL MAGIC
## WORD LIST FOR RÉSUMÉS

## ADJECTIVES

| | | |
|---|---|---|
| Academic | Executive | Qualified |
| Accurate | Extensive | Quick |
| Adaptable | Flexible | Refined |
| Adept | Honest | Reliable |
| Administrative | Idealistic | Responsible |
| Ambitious | Independent* | Self-assured |
| Articulate | Innovative | Self-confident |
| Attractive | Inquiring | Self-reliant |
| Bright | Instrumental | Sensitive |
| Capable | Intelligent | Sharp |
| Challenging | Knowledgeable | Skilled |
| Competent | Leading | Sophisticated |
| Conscientious | Meticulous | Strong |
| Cooperative | Motivated | Successful |
| Creative | Natural | Superior |
| Dependable | Objective | Tactful |
| Detailed | Organized | Technical |
| Diverse | Outstanding | Trustworthy |
| Dynamic | Perceptive | Uncommon |
| Effective | Pioneering | Unique |
| Efficient | Pleasant | Versatile |
| Energetic | Precise | Vigorous |
| Enthusiastic | Professional | Well-groomed |
| Exacting | Proficient | Well-liked |
| Exceptional | Punctual | Well-spoken |

(*Beware: this is one word that scares corporations)

CHAPTER

# 6

## DRESS LIKE A LOW-PAID SECRETARY AND YOU'LL ALWAYS BE TREATED LIKE ONE

### BUTTONED-DOWN EXECUTIVES

There is very little individuality in the clothes that most women wear to the office. Most female executives wear man-tailored suits, man-tailored blouses and running shoes (at least in New York where I work). The result is a legion of fashion clones who obviously think that to be treated equally with men — you've got to dress like them.

Although I regard myself as a good dresser, I wouldn't dream of trying to give someone else advise on the subject. The truth of the matter is that there is no one correct way of dressing. Some women can wear very bright and flamboyant clothes and look stunning — while other women in the exact same attire would look ridiculous. What I can tell you is: WHAT NOT TO WEAR TO THE OFFICE.

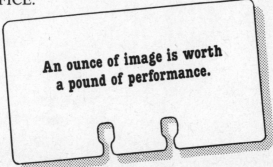

An ounce of image is worth
a pound of performance.

# WHAT NOT TO WEAR

The Hippie Look

The Fredericks of
Hollywood Look

**The Punk Look**

**The Designer Look**

**The Country Bumpkin Look**

**The Harriet High School Look**

**The Jogging Look**

I ♥ ROCK and ROLL

67

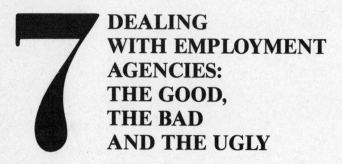

CHAPTER

# 7 DEALING WITH EMPLOYMENT AGENCIES: THE GOOD, THE BAD AND THE UGLY

## WANTED: A TRUTHFUL JOB AD

There are two types of employment ads that appear in the classified section of the newspapers: the ones that are placed by the prospective employers themselves (which are covered later in this chapter) and the ones that are placed by employment agencies. In either case, a good rule of thumb is this: **IF THE JOB DESCRIBED IN THE AD SOUNDS TOO GOOD TO BE TRUE, IT PROBABLY IS.** There are laws which forbid this practice (commonly referred to as Bait and Switch Laws), but they are rarely enforced.

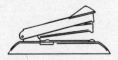

## THE AGENCY EXPERIENCE

Usually frustrating, often degrading and generally a waste of time are three ways I would describe the employment agency experience. I used to think it was just a curious coincidence that so many agencies were so similar in this regard. Now I know why. The entire agency experience is intended to prepare you for the even more dehumanizing experience of getting a job. Let me show you how this works.

68

## STEP I — THE AD

### *What Really Happens*

Employment agencies are really in the cattle business. The more cattle they have at the start of the drive, the more they get to market. Consequently, it is in the agency's interest to devise job ads that will draw the maximum number of applicants. Don't bother to call them on the telephone, they won't tell you anything until you come in, in person.

### *Why They Do It*

You will find that the job ad you answered has as little in common with the job you actually get as the job you get bears to the job description you are given when you take the job.

## STEP II — THE AGENCY'S LOCATION

### *What Really Happens*

Most of the agencies I've gone to are located in a dingy office in some old run-down building.

### *Why They Do It*

This is obviously intended to make you feel that any job is a step up from here

## STEP III — THE AGENCY RECEPTIONIST

### What Really Happens

Like an airport public address system, the receptionist just keeps repeating over and over, "Every applicant must fill out a survey form and be registered before they can see an employment counselor." (P.S. — Doesn't it make you wonder how the receptionist wound up with such a lousy job with all of the great openings supposedly available through this agency?)

### Why They Do It

The message here is obvious — "Don't let this happen to you!"

## STEP IV — THE SURVEY FORM

### What Really Happens

The survey form is nothing more than a restatement of every question that you've already answered (in much greater detail) in your résumé. The logical person may ask, "Why can't I simply give them a copy of the résumé rather than going to the time and trouble of filling out this stupid form?" Don't ask.

"LIST FAVORITE HOBBIES, LIST ADDRESSES OF ALL RESIDENCES THAT YOU'VE HAD IN THE LAST TEN YEARS..."WHAT THE HELL DOES THIS HAVE TO DO WITH GETTING A JOB?

### Why They Do It

This exercise is intended to prepare you for the fact that 90% of your job-seeking time will be spent filling out duplicate forms. (Just think of the millions of hours that could be saved if every corporation and employment agency adopted the same application form, but that would be much too logical.)

## STEP V — THE INTERVIEW

### *What Really Happens*

As you can see, what you thought was going to be the first step is actually the fifth step. At this point, you meet someone called "Your employment counselor." Her/his job is to quickly review your credentials and determine your "employability" (which at some agencies means that the applicant is still warm and breathing).

TWO YEARS OF COLLEGE--FIVE YEARS OF SECRETARIAL EXPERIENCE--GOOD SKILLS ARE ALL FINE, BUT DO YOU MAKE A GOOD CUP OF COFFEE?

EMPLOYMENT COUNSELOR

### *Why They Do It*

It takes an employment counselor only five minutes to review what you've done during the past 20 years of your life. It takes her/him only 30 seconds to decide what you should be doing during the next 20. This is the agency's way of preparing you to be treated as a non-person when you get out into the Wonderful World of Work.

## STEP VI — THE JOB LEAD

### *What Really Happens*

At the end of the interview, the job counselor thumbs through a thick card file of job openings (which I believe still includes jobs that were filled around the turn of the century) and declares, "I've got a few things here that are just perfect for someone with your qualifications."

I'VE GOT THE PERFECT JOB FOR YOU.

WANTED: MALE-- AT LEAST 7 FEET, 5 INCHES-CAPABLE OF LIFTING HEAVY MACHINERY.

### *Why They Do It*

The fact that the job the counselor wants to send you out on bears no relationship whatsoever to your previous experience or stated career goals is the agency's way of telling you that there is no such thing as a "perfect job."

## STEP VII — THE SKILLS TEST

### *What Really Happens*

You will be asked to take a typing and/or stenography test to determine your speed and accuracy (and so that the agency will know how high they can inflate the numbers when they lie about you to potential employers).

### *Why They Do it*

Don't worry that you are nervous or that the test is being administered on a typewriter built in 1455 by Johann Gutenberg — just look at it this way, the jobs that require a lot of typing and steno are probably the jobs that you wouldn't want anyhow.

## STEP VIII — THE TELEPHONE FOLLOW-UP

### *What Really Happens*

A good employment agency will keep an active file of its job applicants and call them several times a week as openings become available — that's what's *supposed* to happen.

### *Why They Do It*

Every 13 weeks you'll get a call asking if you're "still looking"; he says he's got something that's absolutely perfect for you (and the 87 other people he called). It's being the personal assistant to the ambassador of the Palestine Liberation Organization (. . . perfect job if you don't object to an occasional car bomb).

# THE POSITIVE SIDE OF EMPLOYMENT AGENCIES

## SOME OF MY BEST FRIENDS ARE

In fairness, there are a number of agencies who are quite good at helping people find a good job. There's only one reliable way I know to locate these agencies and that's through personal recommendations. You can look at other indicators like the length of time an agency's been in business or the number of complaints listed against them with the Better Business Bureau or the Consumer Affairs Office, but nothing beats the recommendation of a friend who has actually used the agency.

If you can't get a personal recommendation, the next best thing is to call up the personnel directors of the companies that you'd like to work for and ask them who they use. (Don't be surprised if they encourage you to apply directly to them rather than going through an agency.) Once you've got the name of a good agency (and preferably the name of a specific counselor at that agency), call up and say that Ms./Mr. So and So at the Whooziewatsit Company (i.e., the personnel director you just spoke to) suggested that you call and set up an interview.

If you decide to use the services of an employment agency, here are some suggestions about how you can get the most out of that experience:

**(1) KNOW EXACTLY WHAT YOUR JOB OBJECTIVE IS BEFORE YOU GO IN FOR THE AGENCY INTERVIEW.**

**(2) TREAT THIS INTERVIEW LIKE A JOB INTERVIEW BECAUSE THE MORE EMPLOYABLE A COUNSELOR BELIEVES YOU ARE, THE HARDER SHE/HE WILL WORK TO FIND YOU A JOB.**

**(3) LET THE COUNSELOR KNOW THAT YOU'RE EAGER TO FIND A JOB AND YOU'RE PREPARED TO ACCEPT THE RIGHT OFFER IMMEDIATELY IF IT COMES ALONG.**

**(4) CONSIDER THE POSSIBILITY OF OFFERING THE COUNSELOR A SMALL BONUS OVER THE NORMAL FEE IF SHE/HE PLACES YOU.**

## WHAT A GOOD AGENCY CAN DO FOR YOU

✔ *Help you to find a job quickly when you need one right away.*

✔ *Help you to understand the realities of the marketplace (but don't let them undervalue your worth).*

✔ *Prevent you from wasting your time with employers who have bad reputations or who practice discrimination.*

✔ *Help you to focus on the job possibilities in a particular field, especially if it's an agency that specializes in that job field.*

✔ *Give you some pointers about interview techniques or resume writing.*

✔ *Act as the liaison between you and prospective employers when you want to keep your job hunt a secret from your present employer.*

✔ *Help to screen out job interviews that would only be a waste of time given your level of experience or career goals.*

There's nothing more restful than taking orders from fools.

## WHAT'S THE DIFFERENCE?

EMPLOYMENT AGENCY — A company that receives a fee from either the employer or the employee if the employee is actually hired on the basis of their affiliation with both parties.

EXECUTIVE SEARCH FIRMS (THE "HEADHUNTERS") — Usually work only for employers and often receive a fee whether or not they are the ones who actually locate the individual who is ultimately hired for the position. (Most of these companies tend to be extremely specialized by industry and deal only with jobs $25,000 and up.)

EXECUTIVE CAREER COUNSELORS — These tend to be small firms or individuals who, for a fee, will assist an individual in areas such as résumé preparation, interview technique, psychological testing, etc. Executive career counselors will do everything for you with one exception: they won't help you find a job.

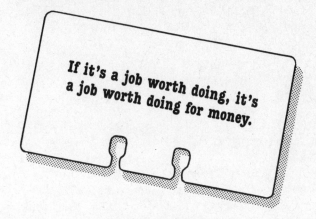

If it's a job worth doing, it's a job worth doing for money.

## BLIND ADS

Ads that direct you to submit your résumé directly to the newspaper or magazine that ran the advertisement or to a post office box number are generally referred to as "blind ads." These ads are usually placed by employers who wish to remain anonymous for any one of several good reasons.

When responding to these ads, try to hook the employer's attention with an impelling cover letter. The best letters are the ones where you can simply say, "You're looking for an administrative assistant with four years experience in banking, and I've got it." The unfortunate reality is that most of the time these letters are not read by the person who will ultimately decide who gets the job — and even it they are, it's hard to distinguish yourself from the other applicants. Here are a few tricks:

• Send it registered mail.

• Answer an ad even if you lack some of the specific job requirements. It's just possible that the company will see something in your résumé that will pique their curiosity and grant you an interview.

- As a last resort there's the "dirty tricks" technique. This involves having a friend send in a résumé which meets every job requirement perfectly. When the company responds to her/him use the information to respond to the company directly.

## OFFICE TEMPORARY WORK, THE BACK DOOR TO SOME GREAT JOBS

One way to find a job that is almost always overlooked is by starting out as an office temp. One of the very best jobs I ever landed came about because I was working for a company on a temporary basis during the extended illness of one of its regular employees. Since the job was by definition only temporary, I experienced none of the nervousness or anxiety that would normally accompany starting a new job. Apparently, this worked to my advantage because after only a week of temping, I was offered a full-time position.

---

### LOOKING FOR MR. GOODJOB

The following is a list of the methods used by employed workers to seek another job.

| | |
|---|---|
| Applied to employer directly | 69.9% |
| Asked a friend or relative | 17.9% |
| Used public employment agencies | 10.4% |
| Used private employment agencies | 5.5% |
| Placed or answered ads | 25.3% |
| Other | 8.2% |

Source: Bureau of Labor Statistics 1976 study.

---

When you think about it, temping is really an ideal way for both the employer and the employee to evaluate one another without either party having to make a commitment. Some employers like to use temps because it frees them from any obligations to pay employee benefits such as sick pay, pensions, etc. (As my mother used to say so indelicately about my live-in lover, "Why should he pay for the cow when he can get the milk for free?") But most employers only use temps in an emergency, as a substitute for a sick or vacationing employee or as a stop-gap measure during the time that they are interviewing new employees.

If you're offered a permanent position while you're temping, the employer will probably have to pay your temporary agency a finder's fee (this means that the company is no worse off than if they had gone through an employment agency in the first place).

I believe that working as an office temp can be an excellent back-door approach to some very desirable jobs.


## A FINAL WORD ABOUT — WHAT ELSE? — MONEY

Employment agencies work in one of three ways:
(1) You pay the fee.
(2) The company that employs you pays the fee.
(3) The employer and employee split the fee.

Maybe I've been lucky, but I've never taken an interview for a job where I was expected to pay the fee. Normally, the agency ads contain phrases like "fee paid" or "no-fee" to identify the fact that the fee is the responsibility of the employer. But be careful.

**The application that you fill out might contain contractual language obligating you to pay the fee. Make sure that each job interview that you take is on a "no-fee" basis.**

**If you do pay the fee, be careful that you only obligate yourself for the period of time that you actually work (otherwise, it's possible to quit a job after two weeks and still have to pay an agency its fee).**

CHAPTER

# 8

# A WORD ABOUT COLLEGES, SECRETARIAL SCHOOLS AND OTHER PLACES WHERE YOU CAN WASTE A LOT OF TIME AND MONEY

## GO TO COLLEGE, BUT...

Let's get rid of the obvious stuff right away — if you can afford to go to college (both in terms of time and money), you'd be a fool to pass up the opportunity. It's also common knowledge that a college degree isn't the passport to fame and fortune that it used to be.

## ANY BLUNDERING IDIOT CAN GRADUATE FROM COLLEGE THESE DAYS

During the past year, one out of every four college graduates took a job below her or his qualifications level. Many women who expected to be ushered into the corporate board rooms upon graduation are disappointed to find that the only positions open to them are secretarial. Some firms even insist that their receptionist be a college graduate. From the company's point of view, this makes good sense because a person's first contact with a company usually comes about through her/his meeting with the receptionist. Unfortunately, this strategy rarely works because most women who are motivated enough to go to college in the first place are likely to want more out of life than the intellectual challenges of being a receptionist. My first job was being a receptionist and I remember spending most of my time at the front desk calling employment agencies and answering classified ads in order to arrange interviews for a better job.

# THE CARROLL COLLEGE THEORY

## FOR THIS I WENT TO COLLEGE?

According to statistics compiled by the U.S. Department of Labor, there is actually a greater earnings gap between men and women who have college degrees than exists between men and women who don't have college degrees. A man who earns a bachelor's degree can anticipate that his median salary will be approximately $20,000. A woman with the same credentials can expect to earn only around $12,000. It is only when the woman continues her education into graduate or professional school that she can expect to close this earnings gap. Naturally, the woman who has her bachelor's can expect to earn more (approximately $3,000 per year) than the woman who doesn't. But these statistics don't tell the whole story.

When the government compares women with a college education to women without a college education it is generally analyzing two entirely different populations of working women. What would be interesting to measure is this: what would happen if you compared two women with identical talents and drives, one who joined a company immediately upon graduation from high school and the other who joined the same company four years later with a degree from an average college?

## HORIZONTAL MOBILITY

Although I can't substantiate this with any empirical data, it is my belief that the woman who took four years out of her life to get her degree will never be able to catch her counterpart who had the four-year headstart in the business world. Naturally, there are exceptions: for example, if the job field that these women enter requires certain technical skills (like being an engineer or a chemist), or if the promotional procedures are strictly regulated (like civil service jobs), then the woman who has the college degree will ultimately be in a more favorable position.

## "WILL ALL THE WOMEN WITH B.A.'s PLEASE LINE UP FOR THE TYPING TEST."

Most companies that I am familiar with hire only a handful of graduating seniors for their executive trainee programs each year. Since twice as many men as women will be hired, the average female college student should face the reality that if she is not at the top of her class or going on to graduate school, she should probably anticipate that she will not be given a managerial level position. I believe that the average woman could improve her odds of breaking into management by going to work for a company directly out of high school. She should spend the next few years building up her experience and contacts (and she can always go to college at night at the company's expense). In the long run, I believe the woman who follows my strategy will be financially much better off. But once again there's an exception

> *I believe that the woman who graduates from a "good" college (even at the bottom of her class) has a tremendous advantage over the woman who graduates from an ordinary college (even toward the top of her class).*

## "GOOD COLLEGES"

What constitutes a "good" college is often only peripherally related to the academic standards of a specific institution. Obviously the Ivy League, Little Ivy and Ivy-caliber colleges (e.g., M.I.T. or Stanford) are all "good" colleges. For everyone else it depends solely upon reputation. Some universities have good reputations

# OVERWORKED AND UNDERPAID

simply because their alumnae and alumni dominate the executive ranks of the important companies in a particular state. Others live off the prominence of one good college within the university or from a school reputation that may have been achieved in another era and is no longer deserved. Still other colleges are regarded as "good" colleges because of their current chic value or because they are a haven for blue-bloods (albeit dumb ones). But most "good" colleges have justifiably earned their notoriety because they can usually be counted on to consistently produce bright, articulate young people who have the potential of becoming successful corporate executives.

## SOME FREE ADVICE (WHICH IS WHAT IT'S WORTH)

Many people stuck in a job rut think they can overcome their inertia by going back to college. Sometimes it works, sometimes it doesn't. When it doesn't, the person has made a costly mistake in terms of time and money (and it could put that person into a psychological tailspin from which she/he may never recover).

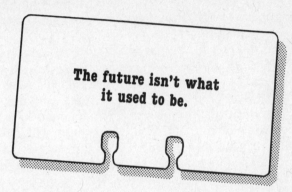

The future isn't what it used to be.

## DON'T ASSUME THAT GOING BACK TO COLLEGE IS THE ANSWER TO YOUR PROBLEMS

In many situations it isn't. The critical thing is to target what your job goals are and then arrive at a strategy for attaining them. If you are currently a secretary and want to move into middle management, you may have to earn a college degree. On the other hand, there are probably a number of people who are currently in management who didn't go to college. Talk to them, find out how they did it. Chances are they'll be very receptive to someone like you who can fully appreciate the magnitude of their achievements. They may even be willing to help you.

## DON'T RELY ON ANY SINGLE STRATEGY TO YIELD THE RESULTS YOU DESIRE

Even if someone is willing to help you — you should always develop a good back-up plan. As a general rule, I usually figure that out of every ten things I hope will happen, only one actually does. Therefore, you should never assume that just because your boss said he would recommend you for a job that you can afford to sit back and wait until it's offered. A million things could go wrong: someone more qualified than you might want the job; someone less qualified but with more clout than you might want the job; your boss could be fired. *One key to success is to have an alternative plan.* Take a course; participate in a workshop; volunteer for a committee; become active in politics. Just do something that will increase your contacts and move you closer to whatever it is that you want to do with your career.

## OTHER ALTERNATIVES

There are many jobs that require more than a high school diploma but less than a college degree. If the job you prefer falls into this category you should find out what the requirements are and which special school programs are most highly-considered by the professionals in that field.

If, for example, you want to become a medical technician or a computer programmer — there are institutes and technical schools which specialize in these areas. It's also possible that you can get the training you require at a community or junior college, or through adult education courses. If you are financially strapped, you should consider alternatives like learning a skill in the armed forces or becoming involved with a government-sponsored training program. The bottom line is this: if you need some training to get ahead there *are* opportunities available for you to get that training.

Don't believe everything you believe.

## THE CPS EXAMINATION

Since 1951 the Professional Secretaries International Organization (formerly known as the National Secretaries Association) has administered an examination known as the Certified Professional Secretary Examination. If a person passes this test and has certain education and work experience requirements, she/he can be granted CPS certification.

I think this program is a good approach to improving the status of secretaries because it tells an employer that this particular applicant has attained a certain status as a professional secretary. Apparently the CPS program works because secretaries who have achieved this credential typically make several thousand dollars more per year than those who don't have it.

The two day examination is administered each May by PSI and covers six parts: behavioral science in business, business law, economics and management, accounting, communications applications, and office administration and technology.

For additional information and an application write to:

Professional Secretaries International
2440 Pershing Road
Crown Center 610
Kansas City, MO 64108-2560

## $ECRETARIAL $CHOOL$

When I graduated from high school the most popular career choices for women were:

1. SECRETARIAL SCHOOL
2. NURSING SCHOOL
3. COLLEGE
4. GETTING MARRIED

Today there is much less emphasis placed on a secretarial school education.

One thing that hasn't changed is that the top secretarial schools, like Katharine Gibbs, do a good job of preparing their students for secretarial careers. The drawback is that the tuition at these schools can cost anywhere from $1,000 to $6,000. If money is no problem, this type of program is sensational because it practically guarantees that you'll receive a good job offer upon graduating. If, on the other hand, it's going to be a struggle for you to pay these fees, I think you have to give some serious consideration to the question of whether or not secretarial school is worth the investment of your time and money.

## TYPE-CASTING

In screening employees for secretarial positions the first question usually asked is, "How well do you type?" (...even though most bosses wouldn't know 60 wpm from 60 mph). The second is "Can you take shorthand?" And the third question (which is being asked with increasing regularity) is "Do you know how to operate a word processor?" Fortunately you don't need to go to secretarial school to learn any of these skills.

I learned to type without ever taking a lesson, and I can type 85 words per minute with few or no errors. Today you can learn to type by video cassette, by computer or through the more traditional sources like YM-YWCA or adult education courses (and all are considerably cheaper than secretarial school).

## SHORT-HANDED

Shorthand can also be learned quickly and inexpensively. The question is, do you want to? While good typing skills are indispensible — there are many interesting jobs available that don't require shorthand. (One study conducted by the University of West Ontario found that most companies who require applicants to pass shorthand tests often don't use shorthand as part of their normal office procedures.) Although I can take shorthand, I find in most dictation situations that I can get by with a fast long hand. If the job requires a considerable amount of shorthand I usually figure that it's likely to be a pretty boring job and I don't bother to apply. Learning to use a word processor is easy and important (see Chapter 14). And there's something else that makes it pretty attractive — jobs that require it usually pay $1,000 to $2,000 more than jobs that don't.

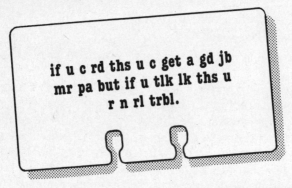

## PENCIL SHARPENING 201

In addition to typing, shorthand and word processing, secretarial schools purport to be able to teach their students everything else they need to know to become good secretaries. There are courses with names like "Business Communications" (i.e., letters and reports), "Secretarial Procedures" (i.e., telephone and filing) and "Professional Development" (i.e., how to dress and talk). While these courses can probably teach you the basic aspects of these procedures, I believe that these things can best be learned in the office rather than the classroom.

## UNCOMMON SENSE

No matter how thorough a secretarial school curriculum is — there are very few graduates who are capable of stepping into a job without some amount of on-the-job training. A secretarial school can show you the basic form of a business letter — but it can't show you how to adapt it to suit each and every different office situation. A secretarial school can demonstrate the proper telephone technique but it can't show you how to deliver it with warmth and personality. And then there are the things that no secretarial school can teach you like how to interact with people, how to create a sense of priorities, how to deal with office politics and how to be the kind of person that other people like and respect. Collectively I refer to these traits as a person's uncommon sense.

*I believe that being a great secretary is 15% skills and 85% uncommon sense.* If you weren't born with a liberal amount of uncommon sense — don't despair. You can't take a course in it ( . . . I take that back; you can take a course on any subject these days!) You can't discover it in some "How-To" book ( . . . although this book will get you closer to it than most). But it can be learned. The trick is simply to observe what successful people do — and follow their lead.

## SEND IN THE CLONES

Be advised that all people imbued with uncommon sense do not all act the same. Some are aggressive, some are laid back. Some are extremely bright, some have just average intelligence. But most successful people do seem to have certain shared characteristics: they tend to be people who are self-confident, people who are risk-takers, people who get a sense of fulfillment from their work, people who have some sense of vision about the future, and most of all, people who like other people.

## THE MORON THEORY OF SUCCESS

You may be saying to yourself, "Hey I know somebody who's terrifically successful, and she/he has none of those characteristics!" Just as there is no accounting for taste, there is also no accounting for success. Anyone with the right amount of capital and/or connections and/or good timing can be a millionaire or the president of a major corporation. Here's the way I look at it:

> *Whenever I meet some obnoxious or*
> *arrogant person who has become rich or*
> *achieved a certain degree of status or*
> *success, I become inspired. I say to myself*
> *"If that moron can go this far, imagine what*
> *I can do!"*

# 9

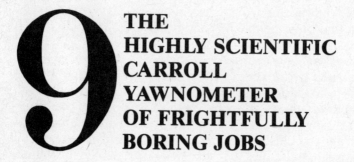

# THE HIGHLY SCIENTIFIC CARROLL YAWNOMETER OF FRIGHTFULLY BORING JOBS

## NEON PEON

As many employment agency counselors will tell you, nothing brings more responses than an ad for a job in one of the so-called "glamor industries" (e.g., fashion, media, entertainment). The allure is not hard to understand; given the choice between working for a re-insurance company or working for a television station, most people will pick the medium over the tedium.

## THE BOZO FACTOR

I'm sure it's no revelation that many of the glamor jobs are not very glamorous and often involve the same amount of routine, schlep work and frustration as any other job. (Believe me, I know!) In some ways they can actually be worse. This is due to what I call the BOZO FACTOR.

### THE BOZO FACTOR
**The more unstructured a business is —
the larger the number of insecure, neurotic
bozos you'll find working there.**

The first corollary of the BOZO FACTOR is that *the number of bozos decreases in direct proportion to an increase in the size of the business.* Consequently, it's much better to work for CBS than it is to work for a small television production company. Not that you won't encounter some flamers at CBS — you will. But the really strange people can't flourish for long in the buttoned-down corporate world of a television network.

Unfortunately, it's the small companies (the ones that spawn the largest number of bozos) that afford a young person the best opportunities to learn the particular business. In a small advertising agency, small music management firm or small independent film production company you can get real hands-on experience plus an exposure to all aspects of the field that you could never get in the compartmentalized world of large corporations.

*And this is one time that women with secretarial skills actually have an advantage over men because there are virtually no entry level positions for males who have no experience.* The problem is that the bozos who run these companies are aware of the fact they have something valuable to offer, and they usually seek to take full advantage of the situation.

It's been Monday
all week today.

## WARNING: WORKING FOR BOZOS CAN BE HAZARDOUS TO YOUR HEALTH

One of my friends worked for a short time as the receptionist/secretary/production assistant/et al. for an independent film production company in New York. The company was owned and operated by two individuals who had worked together for several years and had been fairly successful. Although she was warned by the wife of one of the partners that these guys could be hard to get along with, she figured, "How bad could it be?" She found out pretty quickly.

## LOOKING AT BOOBS — WORKING FOR BOOBS

Apparently, the work technique of this particular office involves abusive verbal assaults by the principals on each of their employees and on each other. During the one day she was there, my friend broke up a fist fight, witnessed a number of large breasted women parading around the offices stark naked (the company specialized in soft porn) and experienced an atmosphere of hostility one might expect in a maximum security prison. My friend desperately wanted film production experience, but fortunately even desperation had its limits.

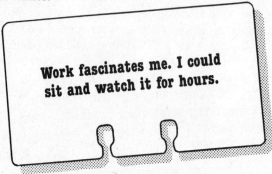

Work fascinates me. I could sit and watch it for hours.

I don't mean to paint an overly bleak picture of the smaller companies within the entertainment industry. The guys my friend worked for were probably aberrational. In all likelihood the worst you'll encounter is a guy with his shirt opened to the third button, wearing more gold chains than Mr. T, trying to make you work very long hours for very little pay. There's no use complaining,

## AVERAGE SECRETARIAL SALARIES OFFERED IN NEWSPAPER HELP WANTED ADS SURVEYED

|  | 1981 | 1982 | Percentage Increase/ (Decrease) |
|---|---|---|---|
| Administrative Assistant | $16,487 | $17,770 | 7.7% |
| Administrative Secretary | 17,294 | 18,248 | 5.5 |
| Executive Secretary | 16,368 | 17,865 | 9.1 |
| Secretary | 14,922 | 15,634 | 4.7 |
| Secretary/Receptionist | 12,301 | 12,273 | (.2) |
| Word Processing | 15,270 | 16,761 | 9.7 |

however, because the fact is that if you don't want the job, 314 other people do. And it's not too hard to understand why when you compare the once-a-year Christmas party in the basement of Howard Johnson's that most companies provide to the "bennies" of these jobs (including things like free concert and show tickets, opening night parties, opportunities to meet celebrities, free record albums, and travel to exotic places).

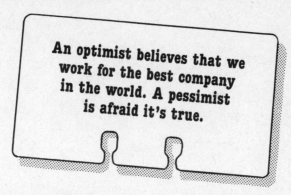

An optimist believes that we work for the best company in the world. A pessimist is afraid it's true.

## THE HIGHLY SCIENTIFIC CARROLL YAWNOMETER

In an effort to help you anticipate how much enjoyment you can expect from any given job, I've assembled THE CARROLL YAWNOMETER which rates jobs from *SOARING* (the best) to *ALLURING* (decent) to *BORING* (mediocre) to *SNORING* (the pits). This highly scientific survey was compiled with the help of some friends over a couple of beers one night.

One thing that everyone agreed on is that *as long as you work for someone else, there's no such thing as an ideal type of job.* There are boring jobs in fun industries and fun jobs in boring industries. Another important thing to remember is that *just because a particular job might be fun — doesn't mean it's going to be fun to work for someone who has that job.* For example, being a lawyer may be a very enjoyable and fulfilling profession, but working for a lawyer is death by Whereas and Wherefore.

So THE CARROLL YAWNOMETER is nothing more than a listing of those jobs or industries where you are most likely to find a position that combines the elements of what I believe most people would consider a great job.

**SNORING**

ACCOUNTING
ACTUARIAL
AUDITING
BANKING
DEBT COLLECTION
DIETICIAN
EMPLOYMENT COUNSELING
ENGINEERING
FLIGHT SERVICE
GOVERNMENT
"HOW TO" BOOK AUTHOR
INSURANCE
LAW FIRMS
LIBRARIAN
MATHEMATICIAN
SECRETARIAL
STENOGRAPHY
TELEPHONE COMPANY
TEXTILES
TYPING
UTILITY COMPANY
WAITRESS

## BORING

AUTOMOBILE INDUSTRY
BARBERING
BARTENDING
CHEF
CONSTRUCTION TRADES
COSMETOLOGY
DENTISTRY
FORESTRY
HAIR DRESSING
HIGH SCHOOL TEACHING
MACHINIST
MANUFACTURING
MECHANIC
MILITARY
PRINTING
REAL ESTATE
RECEPTIONIST
RECREATION
SALES
SECRETARIAL
SOCIAL WORK
TAXI DRIVING
TRAVEL AGENCY
TRUCK DRIVING

**ALLURING**

AIRLINE INDUSTRY
ATHLETICS
COMPUTER PROGRAMMING
COPYWRITING
DANCING
FARMING
FIRE FIGHTING
HEALTH CARE
HOTEL MANAGEMENT
JUDGE
MARKET RESEARCH ANALYSIS
NURSING
PENSION PLANNING
PHARMACY
PHOTOGRAPHY
POLICE WORK
POLITICS
PSYCHOLOGY
PUBLISHING
RADIO
SCIENCE
SECRETARIAL
THERAPY
UNIVERSITIES

## SOARING

ACTING
ADVERTISING
ARCHITECTURE
ARTIST AGENCY
BUYER
CITY MANAGING
COLLEGE PROFESSOR
COMMERCIAL ART
DOCTOR
ECONOMIST
ENTREPRENEUR
FASHION
FILM
MAGAZINES
MODEL
MUSIC
NEWSPAPERS
PUBLIC RELATIONS
RELIGION
SECRETARIAL
STOCK BROKERAGE
TELEVISION
THEATRE
WRITING

# 10

## JOB INTERVIEWS — EVERYBODY'S FAVORITE ACTIVITY (AFTER ROOT CANAL SURGERY WITHOUT ANESTHETIC)

**TEST TIME**

Here's an easy multiple choice question for you:

Which of the following activities do you find most loathsome?

(a) Having your in-laws stay at your house for the entire Christmas vacation?

(b) Turning on the kitchen light and watching hundreds of roaches scurry across your countertops.

(c) Going on a job interview.

(d) Eating calves' brains — and know that you're eating calves' brains.

(e) Taking a shower in an empty house shortly after watching the movie "Psycho."

If you picked (c), the job interview, take solace in knowing that you're not alone. For most people, job interviews are the single most repugnant part of the entire job-finding process. I have friends who openly admit that they would rather stay in a job they despise than submit themselves to job interviews.

## WHAT, ME WORRY?

I consider myself a semigregarious type of personality. Usually I have no problem striking up a conversation, even with people I've just met. But when it comes to interviewing, that's another story. Whenever I had a job interview I always figured that I could count on two things for sure: one was throwing up just before the job interview and the other was throwing up just after it. During the interview I was usually catatonic. A prospective employer could ask me any simple question and I would suddenly find myself with a brain that did not compute and a mouth that was stuck on "hold."

Friends and employment counselors would always give me the same advice: "Relax and just be yourself." That worked fine in theory but miserably in practice.

# RWORKED AND UNDERPAID

## DRUG THERAPY

A friend of mine who had conquered a similar problem told me about her "sure-fire-can't-miss cure." About an hour before an interview she urged me to smoke a big, thick joint. Even though grass is not my thing, I didn't have a job, and I was starting to get pretty depressed so I decided to give it a try.

My first (and last) experimentation with drug therapy took place just before an interview for a job with a major international conglomerate. Since the job involved a substantial increase in salary, I was even more nervous than usual. I thought I'd relieve the pressure by arriving an hour early and toking up in the bathroom on another floor.

## HIGH TIMES IN THE BUSINESS WORLD

Some people have a problem getting high on grass. They sit

around saying dumb things like, "It hasn't hit me yet." Not me. The few times I've tried it I've been up, up and away faster than you can say misdemeanor. But on this particular day I had two tokes — nothing happened. I figured it must be my nervousness, and I took two more. Still nothing. Pretty soon the bathroom had the same pungent aroma as a rock club at 3 a.m. and from the muffled laughter of various women who had periodically come in and gone out again, I figured that "Operation Mellow Out" was no longer a complete secret.

## IT HASN'T HIT ME YET

Soon the entire joint was gone and so was the hour. I couldn't figure out where either of them went, but I was sure that I still wasn't high. I waited till the coast was clear, flushed the toilet for effect and drifted off to the interview. When I was about halfway to the door I was surprised to discover that there was someone else in the bathroom. It was a woman in her late forties with a face pulled tight from years of never smiling. Although the woman was washing her hands in the sink, I was clearly the focus of her attention. Moving her head as slowly as if she were controlling a movie camera, the woman watched me in the mirror until I opened the door and was out of sight.

Time flies when you don't know what you're doing.

## IT STILL HASN'T HIT ME YET

As I rode up in the elevator I remember creating a whole scenario about this woman who had looked upon me so disapprovingly. Mary Margaret McBride. Washed out of the Sisters of Charity in 1961. Went right to work for this company and has been there ever since. Never married. Secretly in love with her boss but wouldn't even entertain the thought of fooling around (after all she and the boss's wife are best buddies).

## IT HIT ME!

As I sat in the reception area waiting to be called I remember thinking to myself, "Well, I didn't get high, but with all of this activity I didn't get nervous either." Eventually, the receptionist told me that it was my turn to go in. I got up, took one step forward — two steps backward, and fell flat on my rear-end. Another woman sitting close by rushed to help me to my feet. The receptionist asked me if I was hurt. I told her I wasn't. I thanked the woman who had helped me and headed down the hall. What I should have said was that I was feeling no pain — boy, was I feeling no pain!

It was a clear case of the old delayed reaction. Instead of walking down the hall, I was gliding. I felt as graceful as one of those horses galloping through the surf in some beautifully photographed commercial. In slow motion. Very slow motion.

My friend was right about not being nervous, but she didn't tell me that I'd be so loose that it would take surgery to remove this dumb smile from my face. For the entire interview I just sat there smiling and nodding, smiling and nodding. As my prospective boss droned on about the joys of working for the company, I found myself constantly drifting away, then tuning back in again a few minutes later. It seemed as if I spent most of the time observing the interview from a spot near the ceiling.

## IF YOU'RE WIRED — YOU'RE HIRED

The biggest surprise of all was that whatever I was doing seemed to be working. At the end of the interview my boss-to-be asked me to go down and meet the company's director of personnel. I smiled one more dumb smile for the road, then floated out of the office.

## IF YOU'RE WIRED — YOU'RE FIRED

I could hardly believe my good fortune. As I rode down in the elevator I couldn't help but laugh at the absurdity of the situation. By the time I got to the Personnel Director's office I was really flying. Then I crashed. The Personnel Director turned out to be none other than ex-nun, sour-faced old Mary Margaret McBride. I don't know who was more surprised. She had me fill in the usual forms and take the usual battery of tests, but we both knew it was strictly a formality. This was one international conglomerate I wouldn't be hearing from — and I never did.

## THE SO-WHAT? APPROACH

I now knew that getting high wasn't the answer, but I still didn't know what was. Then I made a remarkable discovery about myself. I realized that the jobs I was usually offered were the jobs that I wanted least. It occurred to me that when I took the interviews for these jobs I was much more relaxed because I really didn't care whether or not they offered me the job. I wondered whether I could apply this strategy to every interview situation. I decided to give it a try, and to my utter amazement, it worked flawlessly. Here's all you have to do:

*APPROACH EVERY JOB INTERVIEW WITH THE NOTION "I DON'T GIVE A DAMN WHETHER OR NOT I GET THIS JOB."*

I know that sounds like the kind of advice that books like this tend to give, and I know it sounds like something that won't work when applied in a real situation. But think about it this way: statistics show that the average person will remain at a job no longer than 3 years (and if you're a young person, it will be even less).

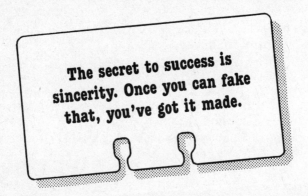

The secret to success is sincerity. Once you can fake that, you've got it made.

If you analyze your own situation — you've probably held several different jobs since you finished school. Each time you took a job I bet you thought, "Now here's a company I could stay with for a long time" or "Here's a job that will really make me happy." But for one reason or another, it didn't turn out that way. And chances are that the next job you take won't be your dream job either. So all you have to do is play the odds and say to yourself, "Since this job isn't likely to change my life forever, why am I getting myself so uptight?" Once you can do it with conviction, you'll be much more relaxed in an interview situation and much less depressed later on if you aren't offered the job.

# PREPARING FOR A JOB INTERVIEW

Not caring about being offered a specific job doesn't mean that you shouldn't be prepared to do your best in an interview. Here are a few tips:

**TRY TO KNOW AS MUCH ABOUT YOUR PROSPECTIVE EMPLOYER AS SHE/HE KNOWS ABOUT YOU.** Some of the ways you can achieve this include:

(a) Call the company a few days before the interview. Find out who you are going to be meeting with and what their position is within the corporation hierarchy.

(b) Read the company's annual report for the past year and any other material that will give you some relevant background information.

(c) For some industries it's possible to obtain a Who's Who or similar type books containing biographical information on prominent individuals in the field. (If, for example, you were interviewing with a law firm, you could check the Martindale-Hubbell directory. It would tell you the names of the schools that your prospective employer graduated from, the date of her/his graduation, and the names of the firm's most prestigious clients.)

**LEARN TO DISTINGUISH BETWEEN A SCREENING INTERVIEW AND A SELECTION INTERVIEW.** A screening interview is intended to eliminate the bimbos and bimbettes and pass along only those most likely to succeed. But if you can't get through the screening interview, you'll never have a selection interview. And if you don't have a selection interview — you don't get hired. So treat both interviews with equal importance.

**NEVER TURN DOWN A JOB INTERVIEW.** Interviewing is like tennis — the more you play, the better you get.

**ARRIVE EARLY.** Don't add to your nervousness by having to rush to get to the interview on time. Plan to arrive with at least 20 minutes to spare and be sure to write down the address and telephone number ( — it's a good little security blanket).

**BE CERTAIN THAT YOUR GOOD REFERENCES ARE GOOD REFERENCES.** If you have any reason to suspect that someone might give you anything less than a fabulous recommendation, don't use them.

**ANTICIPATE THE QUESTIONS THAT YOU MIGHT BE ASKED.** The toughest question that you could possibly be asked is, "Why were you fired from your last job?" Prepare a response that is short, positive, and not at all defensive. Be careful not to speak too disparagingly about your previous employer — no matter what a creep she/he was.

## 10 TOUGH QUESTIONS THAT YOU MIGHT BE ASKED DURING AN INTERVIEW.

Many employers attach as much importance to the way an applicant answers questions as they do the applicant's experience. Therefore, it's important that you think about how you intend to answer questions such as:

1. Why do you want to come to work here? And how did you come to pick this type of business?

2. Do you know anything about me or our organization?

3. What job would you like to have and how much would you like to be earning five years from now? Ten years from now?

4. What experience do you have that qualifies you for this job?

5. Of the jobs that you've held, which did you like the best and which did you like the least? Why?

6. What is your best asset? Your biggest shortcoming?

7. What was the name of the drummer who played with the Beatles before Ringo Starr? (...just wanted to see if you were paying attention.)

8. How do you feel about doing personal work like balancing my checkbook.

9. How do you feel about doing things like getting me coffee, delivering packages or working overtime?

10. And last, but certainly not least, the dreaded open-ended question like, "Tell me something about yourself" or "You can start wherever you want to."

## THE INTERVIEW TECHNIQUE MYSTIQUE

Some "How-To-Find-A-Job" books would have us believe that there is a special technique to giving a successful interview. There isn't. There are no magic clothes to wear or secret words to say. All you have to do is be prepared and be yourself.

Don't make the mistake of trying to act the way you think your prospective employer would want you to act. If you're not comfortable or, worse yet, if you're lying, — it's likely to come across. The people who conduct interviews are usually executives with several years or more of experience. In most cases they can spot a bulltosser at 50 yards. Another reason to be yourself is if this company or this boss has any misgivings about you, your clothes, your ambition etc., it's better to find it out now rather than later.

## SOME SUGGESTIONS ON INTERVIEWING

**A. As soon as you arrive in the interviewer's office, look around for something to make small talk about. "I bet that Woodstock poster is really valuable now, were you there? Or, "I see that you ski — I love skiing." These can be great ice-breakers at the beginning of an interview.**

**B. If you're feeling uncomfortable or nervous, don't be afraid to say so.**

**C. Train yourself to listen to what the interviewer has to say and to make eye contact with her/him at all times.**

**D. Look for an opportunity to let the interviewer know you've done your homework and you're familiar with the workings of the company.**

**E. Keep the interviewer's attention. If you sense that she/he is starting to tune you out — change the tone of your voice, pull some résumés out of your bag — do anything, but keep her/his attention.**

**F.** Carry a copy of a newspaper or magazine that says you are well-rounded (Time, Newsweek, or the Wall Street Journal are perfect) but not so well-rounded (Harpers, Atlantic, etc.) as to be intellectually threatening to the interviewer.

**G.** Don't be afraid to be different (if that's the way you really are!). After a while, applicants start to take on the sameness of wallpaper patterns. If you can stand out, it's to your advantage.

**H.** If the interviewer doesn't seem to be all that familiar with your résumé, look for opportunities to cite your accomplishments.

**I.** Prepare a list of intelligent questions to ask.

**J.** Don't apologize for a lack of experience. Remember you are there to sell yourself first and your experience second.

**K.** Don't act passively because some employers will interpret this as a lack of enthusiasm.

**L.** Have a strong finish. Any good performance demands that you have one. So be sure to save one or two of your greatest hits for your closing statement.

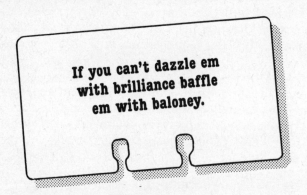

If you can't dazzle em with brilliance baffle em with baloney.

## POST-INTERVIEW ACTIVITIES

One mistake many people make is to think that the interview is the last contact you will have with the company before hearing whether or not you will be offered the job. It doesn't have to be.

If the interview was arranged by an employment agency or a friend — you should follow-up with them. Even if you aren't offered the job they may give you some constructive feedback (like "Go and get yourself a personality lobotomy").

You should send the interviewer a note thanking her/him for taking the time to meet with you.

Try to think of some legitimate basis for following up with the company (like supplying them with a report that you wrote which was a subject of conversation during the interview).

Have one of your references follow-up with the interviewer if that seems appropriate under the circumstances.

If you want to gamble you can try the old gambit, "I hate to pressure you into making a decision, but I was just offered a job with the Nerdski Company and I need to know one way or the other in the next day or two." Just be aware that this strategy can easily backfire on you.

## SUMMARY

If you're stuck in a job rut there's only one way out — you've got to interview for another job. If you have "interview phobia" — the trick is to schedule as many interviews as you possibly can until you get over your fear. Remember only one person can ultimately win the job, so don't be disappointed when you are continually rejected. The more you interview — the better you'll get. Think about it this way: *Many people are locked into dead-end jobs because they are afraid to take risks. If you can at least get up the courage to take that first step and arrange some interviews, you will have given yourself a head-start over 90% of the field.*

This is one chapter that is probably worth rereading.

# 11 TEN QUESTIONS TO ASK BEFORE YOU TAKE THIS JOB — FOR RICHER OR FOR POORER

## THIS COULD BE THE START OF SOMETHING BIG

Here's the scenario: you've followed my advice, got off your buns and started taking interviews. At first you were scared to death but eventually you overcame your nervousness. You adopted the Bridget Carroll "So-what?" approach. In fact you amazed yourself at how self-assured you had become. After meeting with a few more schlubs who were foolish enough to reject you — you hit the jackpot. You've just been told that the job is yours if you want it. You sit there patiently as your prospective boss drones on endlessly about how she/he has watched the company grow from a shoebox to a skyscraper. You sit there nodding, waiting for a chance to talk. Finally (and almost as an afterthought) you are asked, "Do you have any questions?" The answer is a resounding yes because *this will be the last chance you're going to have to set the job parameters that you're going to have to live with forever — or at least until you quit or get fired.*

## SPEAK NOW OR FOREVER HOLD YOUR STENO PAD

The following is a list of the most important items that need to be resolved. Some of these questions may have been answered already — and not all of them should be asked of the boss — the personnel director or employment counselor may be more appropriate. But one way or another, every question needs to be resolved to your satisfaction before you can accept this job.

# A. WHAT'S THE SALARY FOR THIS JOB?

In reality this is probably a moot point since you knew the answer (at least you should have) prior to your first interview. In most instances the salary will be contained in an ad, listed with the personnel department or told to you by the person who set up the interview.

The crucial decisions that you have to make are: what is the job worth? And what are you worth? The simple answer to both questions is: whatever they're willing to pay! However what they're willing to pay might very well depend on what you are willing to ask for. Consequently it's important that you have a good understanding of what the salary range is for a particular type of job in a particular type of industry.

You can find this out by asking people who hold similar jobs (or know people who do) or by checking the classified ads in the

## VERWORKED AND UNDERPAID

newspapers to find out what other companies are offering for this type of position. You can even call the Bureau of Labor Statistics in Washington who compile information such as this.

Determining your own worth is slightly more complicated. A safe rule of thumb in most situations is to use the base salary from your last job and increase it by 15 to 20 percent. (Naturally, this won't work very well if you are moving to a new job field.)

I think most women tend to underestimate their value. Whenever I interview for a job with a predetermined salary range

I usually ask for a few thousand dollars more than the higher number. (You won't lose any points with your prospective employer if you are prepared to substantiate why you feel you are entitled to that salary, and who knows, you may get it.)

---

**THE ART OF
SALARY NEGOTIATING**

Whenever you are negotiating for a higher salary than your prospective employer seems willing to pay......Never say "I want two thousand more per year" — say "The difference between what I'm asking and what you've suggested is only about $39 per week."

Psychologically it's a lot easier for a boss to accept $39 more per week than it is for her/him to accept $2000 more per year.

---

**B.** **WHO HELD THIS JOB BEFORE ME AND WHAT HAPPENED TO HER/HIM?** You should never accept a job until you know exactly what happened to your predecessor. The fact that she/he was fired is not a reason in and of itself to be concerned, but it should make you curious. Another flashing yellow light is a job posted internally that no one seems to want (it's a pretty good sign that the job's a bore or the boss is one helluva sonofabitch).

**C.** **WHAT PERCENTAGE OF THE JOB INVOLVES DOING THE BOSS' PERSONAL WORK?** One of the major reforms urged by those seeking to unionize office workers is the elimination of personal work from the list of a secretary's responsibilities. I say it will never happen; even more importantly, I'm not sure that it should.

*I don't mind doing personal work provided that:*

*(1) I was told before starting the job that it would be expected of me, and*

*(2) I am not asked to do anything that would cause me to be in violation of the company's policies.*

I suppose that making restaurant reservations, balancing checkbooks, planning dinner parties and the like used to be the responsibility of the executive's wife. Now the typical executive's wife is an executive herself. So these days the buck stops at the secretary's desk.

I think I've been lucky because most of the personal things that I've been asked to do over the years have been fun. I've helped to coordinate lavish dinner parties, I've helped to choose artwork and home furnishings, I've shopped for expensive gifts (not for me, of course), I've set up tennis parties, pool parties and surprise parties and of course I've done thousands of other things which haven't been nearly so glamorous. I could have objected (and sometimes if I felt I was being overworked and underappreciated, I did), but if the truth be known — planning a lavish dinner party is a hell of a lot more interesting than typing the sixteenth draft of a real estate lease, that's for damn sure!

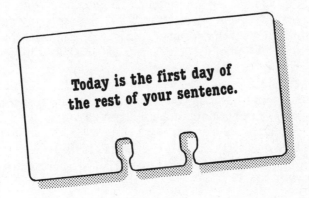

Today is the first day of the rest of your sentence.

**D.** **HOW OFTEN WILL I BE EXPECTED TO WORK AFTER 5 O'CLOCK?** There are some people I know (mostly single mothers) who refuse to take a job that requires them to work past five o'clock. I admire these people for setting a standard and then sticking to it, but I hope they understand they are putting limits on their career potential.

The undeniable truth of getting ahead is that you've got to put in the time. Some of it is just game playing — people who show up early or stay late strictly to be seen showing up early or staying late. But many successful executives stay late or work weekends because that's what's required to be successful.

If you work for somebody who regularly works late, you can expect to see quite a bit of the office cleaning ladies. (Any boss who tells you, "I work late most nights, but naturally I don't expect you to" is plain and simply full of buffalo chips.) In many jobs working past five is a once-a-week proposition — or more. If you're not willing to make this sacrifice, I believe your chances for high salary and rapid advancement will be seriously diminished. Consequently, if you're a working mother, this means you've got to have an understanding husband and/or a flexible babysitter — preferably both.

**E. WHAT IS THE COMPANY'S POLICY WITH REGARD TO BONUSES?** If you work for banks, brokerage houses and other beneficent companies, you will come to understand the importance of the Christmas bonus. The first year you get it, it's pure serendipity, money fallen from heaven. In the second year, you'll have the bonus spent by July.

The bonus can prove to be a substantial portion of your income. In some jobs you can earn as much as 25 percent of your annual salary in the form of a bonus. Although I've never seen any statistics on the subject, I'd bet that more people leave their jobs in January than any other month of the year. The reason is simple: if you leave any earlier, you can kiss that year's bonus goodbye.

So when you are offered a new job, try to include in your new deal whatever bonus dollars you stand to lose by leaving your present company. If they want you badly enough, items like this will not present a problem. But remember, IF YOU DON'T NEGOTIATE IT BEFORE YOU START THE JOB, YOU'LL NEVER GET IT LATER ON, NO MATTER WHAT LIES THEY TELL YOU.

**F. HOW MANY WEEKS VACATION CAN I EXPECT?** Everyone has her/his pet peeves, and vacation time is one of my favorites. I think the 2-week vacation should take its place along side ink pens and green eyeshades as an obsolete office fixture. The 2-week vacation has been around for as long as I can remember. In fact its been around for as long as my father can remember. I think it's time to say "Goodbye and good riddance!"

Because of the state of the economy, airline deregulation and several other factors — airline travel has never been cheaper. But having the money to travel is only half of the equation — having time to travel is the other half. Most people I know use some of their vacation each year to do things like: attend their nephew's wedding in another state, drive their children to college, make repairs around the house or just take a day here and there to preserve their sanity. By the time their 2-week vacation comes along —it more closely resembles an 8-day vacation. If you want to fly to Europe you can expect to lose three days travel time. That leaves leaves you with a leisurely 5 days to see all Europe's sights and splendors. Big deal!

Many executives are entitled to take from 4 to 8 weeks vacation. I specifically chose the phrase "entitled to take" because in point of fact, very few busy executives can afford to take that much time off. But one way or an other, they always seem to be able to "squeeze in" a week of skiing with the family, a week in the islands during the coldest month of winter, and a few weeks at "the cabin" in the summer ( — their idea of a "cabin" looks like my idea of a dream house!)

I think the time has come to close the "vacation gap." Many secretaries put in as many hours as their bosses do and experience as much job-related stress. In return for this commitment, secretaries are rewarded with one-fourth the amount of vacation time that their bosses receive. It's unfair and it's inequitable.

If at first you don't succeed.
Try again. Then quit.
No sense being a damn fool
about it.

Most companies have an established vacation policy. Usually it involves getting one additional vacation day for every year of service or some such baloney. The time to do something about your vacation is *before* you take the job. Tell your boss that you want three weeks vacation to start. The worst that will happen is that she/he will say no (in which case you're no worse off than if you didn't raise it). AND WHEN YOU FINALLY MAKE THE JUMP INTO MANAGEMENT REMEMBER WHAT IT WAS LIKE TO HAVE 2 LOUSY WEEKS OFF OUT OF 52 — AND DO SOMETHING TO CHANGE IT!

**G.** **WHAT IS THE COMPANY POLICY WITH REGARD TO RAISES?** Most large companies have set up a whole series of guidelines as to how and when employees will be evaluated for raises. (Things have improved somewhat from the days of Ebenezer Scrooge and Bob Crachit.) In some cases it's done on an annual basis, in others it's based on the anniversary date of your employment and still others (including many smaller companies) have no set policy at all. It's also important to be familiar with the procedure by which you are evaluated. Is it done strictly by your boss? Do you have an opportunity to talk about your accomplishments before the decision is made? There's only one way to know the answers to these questions — and that's to ask.

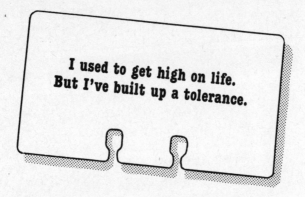

I used to get high on life.
But I've built up a tolerance.

**H.** **WHAT OTHER "PERKS" ARE AVAILABLE?** Throughout this book I have made no effort to mask my displeasure with the way secretaries are mistreated by management. Conversely when management does something which is clearly in the secretary's interest — I do think they deserve to be commended. I hereby award three gold stars to management for their improvement of employee benefits (a.k.a. "perks") such as:

- Medical Plan
- Pension Plan
- Profit Sharing Plan
- Insurance Plan
- College Tuition Reimbursement Plan

Working for a smaller company can have its advantages and its disadvantages. On the minus side, your employer may not provide some basic benefits such as a medical plan. (If you have to pay for it yourself you can figure that a comprehensive medical plan will cost you somewhere around a hundred dollars a month.) On the positive side, the business may be small enough to do things that would be impossible in a publicly-held corporation (e.g., leasing your car through the business so that it becomes a tax write-off).

**I. WHAT KIND OF SCHLEP WORK WILL I BE EXPECTED TO DO?** Notice that the question is not, "Is there any schlep work?" There always is. In fact, you can usually measure a person's importance in a company by the amount of schlep work they delegate to other people.

As long as I'm told before I'm hired what's expected of me and I agree to it, I'll do it. But that doesn't mean I'm going to like it or think it's a productive use of my time. If you're the kind of person who can't stand doing other people's schlep work, then I would suggest working for yourself, joining the groups who are fighting these practices or waiting until you can enter the workforce as an executive.

Check your favorite office nickname:

☐ (A) Honey      ☐ (E) Dear

☐ (B) Sweetie    ☐ (F) Hey, You

☐ (C) Tootsie    ☐ (G) "Office Wife"

☐ (D) My Girl    ☐ (H) None of the Above

**J. WHAT IS THE COMPANY'S POLICY WITH REGARD TO PROMOTIONS?** Don't bother to ask a question like, "Are the prospects for advancement good at this company?" because there isn't an executive in America who will say no. (. . . I mean do you really expect some minion or other protector of the status quo to give you an answer like, "Well no, Miss Carroll, this is a real dead-end job in a real stinkeroo department.") If you want to find out what's really happening, then you've got to learn the answers to questions like these:

(1) Does the company promote from within?

(2) How many women hold important jobs within the executive ranks of the company?

(3) Is there a uniform system of job titles with specific salaries and responsibilities?

(4) How important is a college degree in order to advance to certain positions?

(5) Do they have an Affirmative Action program for hiring and promoting women and minorities?

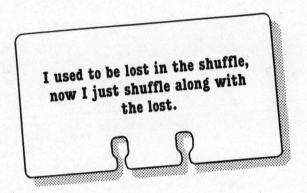

I used to be lost in the shuffle, now I just shuffle along with the lost.

On the question of promotions, I wouldn't be satisfied with the answers you get from your prospective employer. The thing to do is to talk to people who already work for that company. Find out if they're happy. Ask them how closely the company's practices match its policies. If the current employees are satisfied, there's a strong likelihood that you will be, too.

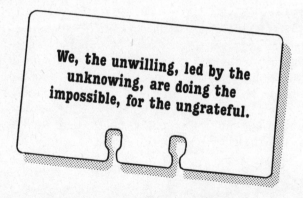

We, the unwilling, led by the unknowing, are doing the impossible, for the ungrateful.

## ONE SECRETARY'S SECRET FANTASY

In the movie "9 to 5" three secretaries got a chance to get even with their tyrannical boss. I think all secretaries harbor similar fantasies. Here's mine.

After months of getting this schtummy's coffee (four times a day) I finally decide I've had enough and tell him to get up and get it himself. He moans and groans until he finally realizes that I'm serious and he has no alternative but to get up and get it. Instead of walking into the kitchen, my boss is such a schtummy that he walks into the closet. Then I get this phenomenal brain-storm.

I rush over and lock the closet door. For the next few weeks every time one of those aggressive, obnoxious office supplies salesmen comes around I tell them that my boss would love to talk with them, lead them to the closet, push them in and lock the door. Pretty tempting, isn't it?

# 12

# HOW TO BE A GREAT SECRETARY (WITHOUT BEING SO GOOD THAT THEY WON'T GIVE YOU A PROMOTION)

## GOOD SECRETARIES ARE AN ENDANGERED SPECIES

One thing that never ceases to mystify me is why so many people perform their jobs so poorly. This is particularly true of many people in the personal service business: waiters are gruff, taxicab drivers are hostile and stewardesses are just downright unfriendly. It's apparent to me that secretaries who possess qualities such as courtesy, efficiency, friendliness and dedication are in very short supply these days. Instead of being depressed by this, I'm elated because it gives those of us who do our jobs correctly the opportunity to shine. I can't remember the number of times that I've received compliments like, "It's such a pleasure to work with someone who does things without having to be asked" or "It's so unusual to deal with someone who is so cheerful."

I think that secretaries who work for middle managers and up are usually competent — the ones who aren't tend to fall into one of these three categories:

## I. SECRETARIES WHO ARE JUST PLAIN OLD DUMB.

These people are generally beyond redemption. Let me illustrate this type by relating a story told to me by a young lawyer who worked for a government agency. In this particular office, the lawyers were required to dictate their correspondence into a dictaphone, which was then sent to a typing pool. My friend swears that on one occasion he got back copies of letters that actually had the words "period," "comma" and "new paragraph" typed right into the body of the letters. Now that's dummmmmmmmb!

**II. SECRETARIES WHO CAN'T HANDLE RESPONSIBILITY.** Almost as bad as the secretary who is just plain dumb is the secretary who thinks she can handle responsibility but can't. A friend of mine was the secretary for a successful Broadway producer named Steve Leber. Leber instructed her to send out telegrams inviting important V.I.P.'s to the opening-night performance of one of his shows. Thinking she could handle this without any further instruction, she sent out the telegrams. She got everything right about the time and place of the show. Even the people with formal titles were properly addressed. There was only one problem. All the telegrams, including those sent to such dignitaries as Canadian Prime

## ERWORKED AND UNDERPAID

Minister Trudeau's wife (who at the time was rumored to be cheating on her husband), were signed "Love, Steve." The secretary is an actress today — and much happier for the change.

**III. SECRETARIES WHO SIMPLY DON'T KNOW WHAT TO DO.** Most incompetent secretaries aren't born that way. They just don't know what to do. If you're interested in becoming a secretary you can spend thousands of dollars on secretarial school or you can take a job and let somebody pay you thousands of dollars while you learn how to do it. It really isn't very hard. Here are some tips, that will help you regardless which alternative you choose.

# HOW TO BECOME A GREAT SECRETARY

(a) **Develop a good phone manner**. The key to developing a good phone manner is to convince each caller that you believe that she/he is important and that her/his problem will be taken care of. All too often the opposite occurs. How many times have you encountered the following conversation?

You: Hello.

Secretary: Hello, Mr. Nerdski's office.

You: Is Nat In?

Secretary: Who's calling?

You: It's Josh Bahbow

Secretary: He's not in right now. May I take a message.

Since the secretary didn't answer the question whether Nerdski was in until after she learned that it was you who was calling, the clear implication is that Nerdski is not in *for you*. The simple way to handle this is to answer the phone: Mr. Nerdski's office, this is Bridget Carroll. Who's calling please? By doing it this way, you not only overcome the problem previously mentioned, but you also get a chance to put in a plug for yourself.

(b) **Improve your skills**. It's not necessary to go to business school to learn to type, take shorthand or use a word processor. All kinds of places from colleges to adult education programs to YMCAs offer these courses. In fact, there is a computer program that teaches you to type, a computer program that teaches you how to take shorthand and even a computer program that teaches you how to work a computer.

(c) **Each morning be sure to review the correspondence before you do anything else** (...yes even before eating your buttered roll or drinking your coffee).

(d) **Create a good filing system**. It doesn't have to work for anyone else but you and your boss. (Make sure that important papers are properly safeguarded.)

(e) **Maintain a tickler file**. There's nothing worse than missing a deadline. Therefore, it's important to set up a file which alerts you to important dates at least a week in advance of those dates.

(f) **Learn to use the OAG** (a comprehensive guide which lists
all airline travel routes). Another good practice is to always
check with airlines to ascertain any changes in flights or fares.
Don't trust travel agents particularly if you are looking for the
cheapest fare: Remember travel agents are paid a percentage
of what you spend so it's not really in their interest to find you
the best deal.

(g) **Assume the validity of Murphy's Law** (*Anything that
can go wrong will go wrong*). If you have to transfer somebody
to another office, give them the extension number ahead of
time so that when you're abruptly cut off, the person will know
what number to re-dial. Likewise when your boss buys theatre
tickets, note down the numbers. (If they're ever lost or stolen —
you can change into your "Super Secretary" garb — and fly to the
rescue.)

(h) **Take advantage of opportunities to learn new things**. As
part of the sales package most manufacturers of word processors
and other office machines offer to train company employees
on how to use their equipment. You'd be foolish if you passed
up an opportunity such as this to learn an important skill for
free. (But be careful not to become too good at any one office
machine or you'll spend the rest of your career hearing people
say things like, "Call Bridget, she knows how to add the
oversized paper.")

(i) **Become adept at recognizing people's names and voices—**
Nothing makes a caller or visitor feel more comfortable than
when she/he is immediately recognized. Whenever you meet
people, try to memorize their name, their face and their voice.
You should also try to learn little pieces of chit-chat you can
use in future conversations (. . .just be careful not to overwork
the same piece of information so you are still asking about

someone's daughter's little league no-hitter — when it's been six years since the kid stopped playing baseball).

**(j) Compare the calender you keep to the one that your boss keeps**—Invariably, your boss will make appointments that you'll never be told about. By checking both calendars on a daily basis, you'll create a failsafe system, and you'll know where your boss is at all times.

**(k) Develop a good rapport with the local typewriter repairman**—Most corporations have service contracts with companies who repair typewriters. When you call for service, you can expect to wait anywhere from three hours to three years. By maintaining a good relationship with the repairman, you can minimize your waiting time and your boss' frustration (because it's a well-established fact that office typewriters only break down just before the deadline for a major report).

**(l) Set up a tickler system of all your boss' most important personal dates including key birthdays and anniversaries**. Keep a number of greeting cards on hand and give them to her/him to send a few days ahead of the appropriate occasion (...and don't forget her/his birthday!).

**(m) Spend some of the company's petty cash to make your office environment more liveable**. Fresh flowers for your boss' office and for your desk is a good place to start.

**(n) Plan for possible emergency situations by storing a bottle of good wine or champagne in your desk drawer.** I guarantee the day will come when your boss will need it to entertain or to serve as the gift she/he forgot to buy.

**(o) Develop a relationship with your boss' husband/wife or live-in-lover.** As a personal assistant, you are likely to spend more time with your boss than they will — and the potential for jealousy is enormous. Therefore, it's extremely important to be as non-threatening as possible.

## WRITING

### LEARNING TO WRITE

Developing a good writing style is helpful if you want to be a great secretary and even more important if you want to advance to a managerial position.

There is a glut of books and courses that purport to be able to teach people how to write. None of these things have ever worked for me. Whatever writing skills I have, I acquired the same way that I learned to play tennis. I watched how the pros did it and then I went out and tried to copy their style.

The filing cabinet at your feet is loaded with hundreds of letters and reports. Study the ones which are well written, then copy their format and style. It's really that simple.

**(p) Establish a network of contacts who can come through for you when the chips are down.** Hotel rooms, concert tickets and Broadway show tickets are the kinds of things that your boss is likely to need only at a time when they're impossible to get. With a little thought, you can anticipate these problems and work them out. (eg., many concert promoters have "ticket clubs" which, for an annual membership fee, allows you to purchase two tickets for any show they produce. I've found that being able to produce an unexpected pair of tickets to the Rolling Stones is more appreciated than working five straight nights of overtime!)

**(q) Learn to identify the types of people your boss really doesn't want to talk to** (like the person from her/his graduating class who's now in the life insurance business).

**(r) Be honest with your boss.** Don't be afraid to tell your boss she/he is dressed like a dortschnagel or that certain things she/he has done or said have offended other people in the office. And if your boss can't take a joke . . . well, you know what they say.

**(s) Think of ways to make your boss look good.** Most bosses like to think of themselves as being very "au courant" (even though most of them are more "au fogey"). You can make your boss look good by telling her/him about "the" new restaurant, "the" new club, "the" new whatever (chances are you won't be able to afford to go there yourself on what you're being paid so you might as well experience it vicariously through your boss). If the place turns out to be a winner, you're sure to score points every time your boss gets to brag to a friend — "Oh yes, I went to that place a couple of months ago when it first opened. I hear it's pretty commercialized now, but you should try it. It's lots of fun."

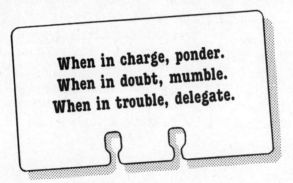

When in charge, ponder.
When in doubt, mumble.
When in trouble, delegate.

**(t) Serve as your boss' personal publicity agent.** When your boss receives a major promotion or accomplishes something noteworthy, get the word out. College alumni magazines and hometown newspapers will usually print whatever you give them verbatim and even run a photograph—so send them one.

**(u) Be a friend to your boss' children.** But be sure you make it clear right from the outset that you are not working for them. And let your boss know it, too, otherwise you'll spend half of your day typing term papers on "The Bears of North America."

**(v) Become a notary public.** It's really simple to do and you'll be surprised at how often it comes in handy.

**(w) Be a good record keeper**. This is particularly important in a small business where your crooked boss is writing off everything from his wife's tennis luncheons to his son's tickets to the Bruce Springsteen concert.

## THE SECRETARIAL FAN DANCE

Few things are as important to master as the Secretarial Fan Dance. The Dance is part of an ancient ritual that has been passed down through several generations of secretaries.

The basic steps of the Dance involve moving quickly from side to side so that you are not hit when the nasty stuff hits the fan. A good secretary will know when it's appropriate to keep dancing and when it's appropriate to get her buns off the dance floor. A great secretary will be able to maneuver her boss' buns simultaneously.

The patron saint of Fan Dancers is Ms. Rose Mary Woods, Richard Nixon's personal secretary during his presidency. As the Watergate investigation started to heat up (and with stuff flying all around her), Ms. Woods did one of the most spectacular Fan Dances ever seen as she sought to explain an 18 1/2 minute gap in a Watergate tape that might have led to the indictment of her boss. For her fancy footwork under pressure, Rose Mary Woods has been named to the Secretaries Hall of Fame (see Chapter 22).

## THE SECRETARY'S REFERENCE LIBRARY

**(Note: Nearly all of the following are currently available as computer programs as well.)**

**DICTIONARY**—Any good unabridged version.
**THESAURUS**—A must so that you don't have to keep repeating the same word over and over and over and over and over.

**OFFICIAL AIRLINE GUIDE (OAG)**—Contains a complete listing of all airline routes and schedules (published by Dun and Bradstreet in New York).

**BARTLETT'S FAMILIAR QUOTATIONS**—A sure-fire way to look smart is to start a report with some obscure quote from some obscure literary figure (published by Little, Brown & Co., in Boston, Mass.).

**INFORMATION PLEASE ALMANAC**—A great one-volume source of facts (published by A&W Publishers in New York).

**RAND McNALLY ROAD ATLAS AND TRAVEL GUIDE** —Even if your boss isn't a salesperson, you'll be surprised at how often you'll use this book (published by Rand McNally & Co. in New York).

**HOTEL AND MOTEL RED BOOK**—This is only valuable when your boss is travelling to a new place. In most cities, past experience or company policy will dictate where your boss will stay (published by American Hotel/ Motel Association Directory Corporation in New York).

**A GRAMMAR AND STYLE BOOK**—There are dozens of good ones on the market. (I have one and still can't figure when to use "affect" instead of "effect".)

## AN INDISPENSABLE
## INFORMATION SOURCE

I feel like a restaurant reviewer who is about to expose the name of a favorite restaurant knowing full well it will probably never be the same again once it has become common knowledge.

Nevertheless, I figure I've got to put something in this book to rationalize the cover price. So let me share a great source with you. Whenever you need almost any piece of information just call (212) 340-0849. It's a service of the New York City Public Library, and it can literally save you hours of time hunting around. And it's absolutely free!

# PROTOTYPE SECRETARIAL JOB DESCRIPTION

A secretary relieves an executive of various administrative details; coordinates and maintains effective office procedures and efficient work flows; implements policies and procedures set by employer; establishes and maintains harmonious working relationships with superiors, co-workers, subordinates, customers or clients, and suppliers.

Schedules appointments and maintains calendar. Receives and assists visitors and telephone callers and refers them to executive or other appropriate person as circumstances warrant. Arranges business itineraries and coordinates executive's travel requirements.

Takes action authorized during executive's absence and uses initiative and judgment to see that matters requiring attention are referred to delegated authority or handled in a manner so as to minimize effect of employer's absence.

Takes manual shorthand and transcribes from it or transcribes from machine dictation. Types material from longhand or rough copy.

Sorts, reads, and annotates incoming mail and documents and attaches appropriate file to facilitate necessary action; determines routing, signatures required, and maintains follow-up. Composes correspondence and reports for own or executive's signature. Prepares communication outlined by executive in oral or written directions.

Researches and abstracts information and supporting data in preparation for meetings, work projects, and reports. Correlates and edits materials submitted by others. Organizes material which may be presented to executive in draft format.

Maintains filing and records management systems and other office flow procedures.

Makes arrangements for and coordinates conferences and meetings. May serve as recorder of minutes with responsibility for transcription and distribution to participants.

May supervise or hire other employees; select and/or make recommendations for purchase of supplies and equipment; maintain budget and expense account records, financial records, and confidential files.

Maintains up-to-date procedures manual for the specific duties handled on the job.

Performs other duties as assigned or as judgment or necessity dictates.

Reprinted by permission. Copyright © 1983, The Secretary, official publication of Professional Secretaries International, Kansas City, MO.

## OTHER INDISPENSABLES

**A Pocket Calculator**—I've never yet worked for a boss who could add — except for an accountant named Arnold (....is that redundant? Aren't all accountants named Arnold?)

**Trade Publications**—What business you're in will determine which annuals, business guides, etc., are indispensable for your industry.

**An Artist Gum Eraser**—This is the thing that looks like a wad of gray chewing gum. I put it on my desk just to watch people pick it up and start molding little clay figures with it. It's irresistible.

**A Chic Book**—If you want to avoid being typecast as a run of the mill secretary, do your trashy novel reading at home. When you're in the office, you should only carry books that have a chic value attached to them. In determining what's chic and what isn't, a good rule of thumb is that the more ponderous or incomprehensible a novel is, the more likely it is to be considered chic. You'll never have to read one of these awful books if you remember to do two things: (1) Read the publicity blurbs on the cover ("This is a book that explodes the myths and fears surrounding. . .") and (2) If anybody asks you what you think of the book simply reply, "I'm having a hard time getting into it, it's definitely not as good as the last novel."

---

### ONE FINAL THOUGHT

Dear Friends:

When you type a letter, do not put your initials in lower case type at the bottom of the letter. And under no circumstances should you ever put your lower case initials next to your boss' upper case initials (...that's a public admission that you're half as important as she or he is).

The simplest solution is to put both sets of initials in upper case letters. I hope you get the idea.

Very truly yours,

*Bridget Carroll*

Mary Bridget Carroll

MBC/MBC

---

124

CHAPTER

# 13

# THE SECRETARY'S WHITE-OUT DIET AND EXERCISE PLAN

## NOTHING GAINED, NOTHING LOST

Some people don't realize how physically demanding a secretary's job can be. In order to help working people cope I have devised an exercise workout and diet plan that fits in perfectly with their daily routine. I call it the White-Out Plan because the objective is to "white out" those extra pounds and unsightly bulges. The nice thing about this plan is that you don't have to do anything differently from your normal regimen. Of course you won't lose any weight, but then how much weight have you ever lost on a legitimate diet and exercise plan?

## EXERCISE WORKOUT
### EXERCISE #1: STAPLE REMOVING

**PURPOSE**—To strengthen and tone thumb and index finger. (This is a good warmup for the more exhausting exercise of phone dialing.)

**TECHNIQUE**—(a) Grasp staple remover with thumb and forefinger.

(b) Line up staple to be removed by inserting points of staple remover directly under staple.

(c) Press and pull.

(d) Now repeat exercise with next stapled document using other hand.

**CADENCE**—Repeat to yourself, "For this I went to school? For this I went to school?"

### EXERCISE #2: ROLODEXING

**PURPOSE**—To limber up one's wrists in preparation for a day of strenuous typing and/or dirty coffee cup washing.

**TECHNIQUE**—Grasp plastic knobs at each end of rolodex and rotate clockwise with fingertips unless (and here's the tricky part so follow along closely) the last card you looked up was Bruno Bagadonuts and the next one you need is Abduhl Yassir — in which case rotate counter clockwise (...it's one of those valuable shortcuts that takes years to master).

**CADENCE**—Boss screeching in staccato fashion, "Get Bruno Bagadonuts, then I want Abduhl Yassir, then I want Ellen Donnelly at Shearson, then get me Ed Meyer, no get me Ed Meyer then get me Ellen Donnelly, then get me..."

# OVERWORKED AND UNDERPAID

STAPLING EXERCISE
A: LIFT ARM
B: HIT STAPLER

I'LL JUST PRETEND IT'S THE BOSS' HEAD.

PHONE EXERCISE
A: WHEN PHONE RINGS, LIFT OFF HOOK
B: WHEN DONE, REPLACE RECEIVER

LUNCH EXERCISE
A: INSERT SANDWICH INTO
B: TAKE BITE
C: PHONE RINGS
D. INDIGESTION BEGINS

### EXERCISE #3: COPYING — COLLATING — HOLE PUNCHING

**PURPOSE**—To improve eye-hand coordination for the more advanced exercises such as watering hanging office plants or defrosting the office refrigerator.

**TECHNIQUE**—(a) Position yourself in front of the copy machine.

(b) Breathe in deeply. If you're doing it correctly you should be able to smell the chemicals used in the toner or feel the ultra-violet radiation (either of which will literally melt the pounds away).

(c) Insert paper. Select the number of copies. (. . .am I going too fast for you?) Push START button. (N.B. If machine fails to operate and flashes the signal "CHECK PAPER TRAYS" walk back to your desk in a quick but unobtrusive manner. Do not call key operator. Adding copy paper is a difficult exercise that should only be undertaken by experienced office exercise enthusiasts.

(d) Lay copied papers out on conference room table. Walk around picking up pages in numerical order (. . . as you can see few exercises combine serious physical and mental training as well as this one does).

**CADENCE**—Any chain-gang or cotton field work song is appropriate.

You can't win.
You can't break even.
You can't even quit.

## EXERCISE #4: CIGAR PURCHASING

**PURPOSE**—This is the best exercise in the workout for cardiovascular improvement because it is the only one that requires a significant amount of physical movement. It is also great for your psychological well-being because you have the pleasure of knowing that even though you are doing something which is an absolute waste of your time — the net result is that you are helping to shorten your boss' life expectancy.

**TECHNIQUE** (a) Your boss puts his feet up on his desk and begins to read the bathing suit issue of Sports Illustrated (for the 14th time this week).

(b) You are seated behind your desk (. . .which is no longer visible under the pile of work that seems to redouble itself like the loaves and the fishes).

(c) Without looking up from Cheryl Tiegs's bikini, the boss calls out to you (in which he regards as his nice voice), "Honey, could you go downstairs and pick me up a couple of cigars?"

(d) You look up and see him sitting there doing nothing while you are working your buns off. You start to feel tremendous anger and contempt welling up inside of you (this is good for blood circulation).

(e) Once again without looking up he barks, "Now!"

(f) You get up, walk out to the elevator and ride down to the lobby to get his lousy cigars.

CADENCE—Follow the bouncing ball and sing: "Working 9 to 5, what a way to make a living. It's enough to make you crazy if you let it."

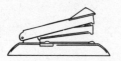

## THE SECRETARY'S DIET

Even the best exercise program is worthless if it's not supplemented by a regular plan of diet and nutrition. The following diet may already be part of your daily routine.

**2:30PM** You look at your watch and realize that you haven't gotten up from your desk once during the past five and a half hours.

**2:35PM** You call and order a chicken salad sandwich from the luncheon restaurant in your building. They say they'll send it right up.

**4:00PM** The sandwich still hasn't arrived.

**4:30PM** The sandwich arrives. It costs you $5.50 for two soggy pieces of white bread with salmonella sauce and a watery ice tea. Plus tip.

**4:31PM** Suddenly your boss is hovering around your desk eyeing your sandwich like a dog eyes a garbage bag. Finally he works up the courage to ask you for, "Just a half." Reluctantly you give it to him. He wolfs it down in one gulp.

**4:32PM** He turns and walks back to his office. Just as you finally lift the sandwich to your mouth, he bellows, "Bridget, I've got some very important letters to get out. . .when you're finished eating. . ."

**4:33PM** You throw the sandwich in the garbage. You get up and walk into your boss' office. You know that by the time you get to drink your ice tea again it will have grown bacteria cultures.

You have now successfully completed your first day of the Secretary's Diet. Total calories — two and a half. Repeat each day Monday through Friday. If followed religiously you're guaranteed to lose 20 pounds in six days and your mind in two weeks. If desired, you may substitute a vending machine candy bar for the chicken salad every other day.

Bon Appetit.

CHAPTER

# 14

## OFFICE AUTOMATION: THE SECRETARY — AN ENDANGERED SPECIES?

### MEET r2d2, YOUR NEW SECRETARY

A great deal of myth and misunderstanding has developed around the issue of how computers will impact upon the role of the traditional secretary. While it's true that computers will profoundly change the job as we currently know it, I think there is little chance that secretaries are in danger of becoming extinct or being turned into keypunch robots.

## OVERWORKED AND UNDERPAID

I CAN'T BELIEVE HOW HARD TERRY IS WORKING SINCE WE PUT IN THAT WORD PROCESSOR.

WAKKA! WAKKA!

In a survey of its members conducted by Professional Secretaries International in conjunction with the Minolta Corporation, it was found that secretaries don't believe that their jobs are in jeopardy as a result of increased office automation (see Table 1).

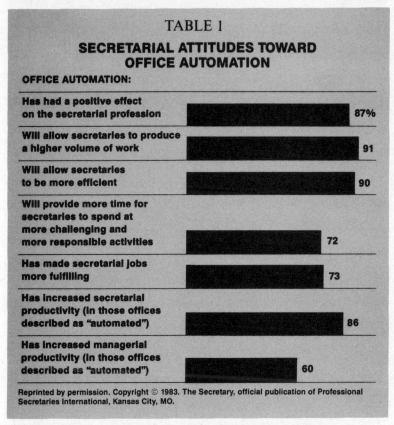

TABLE 1

## SECRETARIAL ATTITUDES TOWARD OFFICE AUTOMATION

OFFICE AUTOMATION:

| | |
|---|---|
| Has had a positive effect on the secretarial profession | 87% |
| Will allow secretaries to produce a higher volume of work | 91 |
| Will allow secretaries to be more efficient | 90 |
| Will provide more time for secretaries to spend at more challenging and more responsible activities | 72 |
| Has made secretarial jobs more fulfilling | 73 |
| Has increased secretarial productivity (in those offices described as "automated") | 86 |
| Has increased managerial productivity (in those offices described as "automated") | 60 |

Reprinted by permission. Copyright © 1983. The Secretary, official publication of Professional Secretaries International, Kansas City, MO.

## ELIMINATING SOME OF THE SCHLEP WORK

I believe that office automation will give secretaries an opportunity to upgrade their jobs while reducing or eliminating many of the time-consuming duties that they find least desirable. Table 2 lists the tasks that are most closely associated with a secretary's responsibilities. As you can see, very few of the jobs considered "most desirable" are threatened by computers. And some of the "least desirable" jobs such as filing can actually be improved by a computer system which allows these tasks to be done faster and easier.

## THE TIMES THEY ARE A-CHANGIN'

America's economy has grown and prospered because of its willingness to assimilate and apply technological change. Office automation is clearly an important part of the next phase of that growth. As Bob Dylan wrote, "Your old road is rapidly agin'. Please get out of the new one if you can't lend your hand. For the times they are a-changin'."*

## TABLE 2

### RATINGS FOR SECRETARIAL TASKS

| | % OF SECRETARIES | | | |
| TASK | Like Very Much | Like Somewhat | Dislike Somewhat | Dislike Very Much |
|---|---|---|---|---|
| Receive Visitors | 78% | 20% | 2% | 0% |
| Write Letters For Executive | 73 | 22 | 4 | 1 |
| Type | 70 | 27 | 3 | 0 |
| Arrange Meetings | 70 | 25 | 4 | 1 |
| Schedule Appointments | 66 | 29 | 5 | 0 |
| Make Travel Arrangements | 64 | 30 | 5 | 1 |
| Attend Meetings | 62 | 33 | 4 | 1 |
| Take Shorthand/ Rapid Note Taking | 49 | 35 | 12 | 5 |
| Answer Telephone/ Route Calls | 46 | 36 | 14 | 4 |
| Open/Sort Mail | 35 | 53 | 10 | 2 |
| Order/Maintain Equipment and Supplies | 29 | 48 | 19 | 4 |
| Photocopy/ Duplicate | 8 | 44 | 41 | 7 |
| File | 7 | 28 | 39 | 26 |

## TERMINALS AREN'T TERMINAL

Learning to use a word processor should not be viewed in the same way that many people have regarded learning to type — *it is not just a secretarial function.* Walk through any large corporation and you'll find computer terminals (commonly called VDTs — Video Display Terminals) on the desks of many of the most important executives. In my business (stock brokerage), a computer is an absolutely indispensible tool for everyone. In fact, it's almost getting to be a status symbol to have more or better computers than the person in the office next to you. *Just remember, in an office setting information is power and knowing how to use a computer is your access to information.*

## THE PRODUCTIVITY TRAP

With such extraordinary changes occurring in the workplace it's not surprising that there have been problems. Bosses, who ironically often pose the most resistance to learning the new technology, usually have very unrealistic ideas about what the machines can do. Christine V. Bullen of the Massachusetts Institute of Technology put her finger on the problem. "What has happened to date is that analysts have looked at office work, and observed the easy, structured, and repetitive tasks. They have been looking at things which are not important, things that are not going to make any significant difference in productivity. Productivity depends on two things: how much time is spent doing a particular task and how important that task is to achieving the mission of the office. People seem to overlook the latter. The majority of the products we have seen so far are not focused on facilitating the tasks which are important to achieving the mission of the office."[1]

## THE NEW SWEAT SHOPS

In an effort to maximize productivity many companies have created word processing departments which are frequently centralized within the office complex. All too often these facilities are run in a rigid factory-like fashion with strict work rules and quotas. Workers in these word processing units are asked to work on pieces of text or sections of legal briefs as though they were bolts to be welded to the tail section of a 747. The result is a bleak, anonymous existence that I wouldn't recommend to anyone.

1. Christine V. Bullen, "Hang On, The Ride Is Just Beginning." THE SECRETARY, June-July, 1983.

# THE ABCs OF OFFICE COMPUTERS

The word processor consists of a number of pieces of equipment called hardware. The most common pieces of hardware are the computer, a video screen (VDT or CRT), keyboard, printer, and disc drive. This hardware can be found in a single unit called a console, or it can come in separate pieces called components. Either way, all the parts are connected by wires, cables and switches.

The heart of a word processor is a computer that has been programmed to handle words. The keyboard can be used exactly the way it is used on a typewriter, or it can be used to give instructions to the computer. When the keyboard is used for typing, the words appear on the screen instead of on paper. At the same time, the words are stored inside the computer. In order to put the words on paper the computer must be given instructions to activate the printer.

The computer "understands" the command to print because internal switches have been preset by a program (which is simply a predetermined set of instructions). Professionals refer to these programs as software.

The fact that the words are stored in the computer means that the computer can be "told" to do many different things with those words. It can delete them, change them around, or it can substitute new words. It can change the format from double spaced draft to single spaced final and back again, all with the touch of a few keys. Moreover, frequently used phrases, paragraphs, letters and other documents can be preserved and then used over and over without retyping.

The ability to save and reuse text is one of the main things that sets word processing apart from typing. This capability is made possible because the word processor has an electronic "memory." The words that are typed into the word processor can be stored in this memory and called back to the screen or sent to the printer whenever needed.

In order to prevent the loss of textual material, all word processors utilize an auxiliary memory system. The most common of these is the "disc drive." This piece of hardware uses a magnetic disc enclosed in cardboard to save text outside the word processor's memory. These discs are made from the same material as the familiar tape in audio cassettes. Like the tape, computer discs can record, playback, and erase information sent to it by the word processor.

## DECENTRALIZATION

Studies have shown that secretarial jobs for people assigned to typing pools turn over three times faster than those secretarial positions where the people are assigned to a specific individual. I think that when studies are done on the workers in these centralized word processing centers the turnover will be even greater. The solution is decentralization. That means each secretary works directly for one or more specific managers with whom she/he has daily contact. Instead of working on a piece of text from which she/he is completely detached — a person in a decentralized office tends to be very familiar with the information she/he is asked to process. That secretary knows the person who wrote it, the person to whom it is being written and where and how to find it when it's needed for some future project.

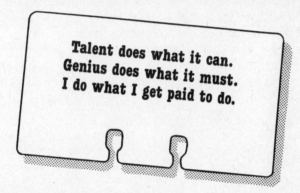

Talent does what it can.
Genius does what it must.
I do what I get paid to do.

## SPEAK NOW OR FOREVER HOLD YOUR PEACE

Since computers can be interactive (which means that they can interconnect with any other computer within the office), it seems to me that there is very little need for the large centralized word processing ghettos. As a secretary you have a lot to lose and nothing to gain if this type of system is implemented in your office. My strong advice on this subject is to use whatever clout you've accrued to see that it doesn't happen. Let your boss know how strongly opposed you are to this type of arrangement — *even if it doesn't specifically effect your particular job.* Another thing you can do is to try to get yourself named to the management team that is studying which types of computer equipment the office intends to buy (. . .after all, you're the one that's going to have to use it — not them!).

## SECRETARITRON

Within the next few years it seems certain that secretarial jobs will be dramatically transformed as a result of computers. Businesses will have computers that respond to human commands, computers that read the printed word and computers that talk to other computers. Some new job categories will be created and others will disappear. I believe that the net effect for secretaries will be positive. I think it will free them from many of the boring parts of their jobs (like filing and retyping the same set of documents) and allow them to concentrate on what they do best — the administration and coordination of the business of that office. As Heather Menzies, who has written two books on the impact of computers in the workplace, says, "Future jobs are not computer jobs so much as information jobs. As professional secretaries, you ultimately are information workers. The most important asset you will have is your understanding of your organization and what it is already doing and, most important, your understanding of the market that it serves. You're dealing with the world outside. Therefore you're in a position to be able to anticipate new ways that these computer systems can be put to use, applying the company's existing product line and information base to create new services and products for your clientele."[2]

2. Heather Menzies, "Scenarios for Restructuring the Professional Secretary's Role," THE SECRETARY, June-July, 1983.

CHAPTER

# 15

# ADVICE FOR BOSSES ON HOW TO PLEASE YOUR SECRETARY

## "MY GIRL"

You've finally found a top-notch secretary. She's poised, intelligent, has a sense of humor, excellent skills — and takes the work as seriously as you do. Congratulations! Now, here's all you have to do to make her happy:

**1**. Always glance at your watch when she arrives in the morning — it'll keep her on her toes. (Exception: when she gets in early, pretend not to notice.)

**2**. Having her serve your coffee is one of the delightful prerequisites of executive life; don't disturb the chain of command by occasionally bringing her a cup.

**3**. Tell her all about your plans for vacationing at St. Tropez. It's the little personal touches that humanize the boss/secretary relationship.

**4**. Don't ask her if she had a nice weekend — she may start to tell you about it, and you have a lot of important things to attend to.

**5**. Dictate your letters right off the top of your head. A good secretary expects to do three or four revisions.

**6**. When she's typing a 25-page document that has to go out by noon, buzz her and ask her to handle some small detail for you. She'll appreciate the change of pace.

**7.** Ask her to do your personal banking. It will give her something to aspire to when she sees your bank balance.

**8.** Refer to her as "my girl." It'll keep her feeling young at heart.

# OVERWORKED AND UNDERPAID

**9.** When she's totaling your luncheon expense record while brown-bagging it with a tuna sandwich, comment enthusiastically on the virtues of home-made food.

**10.** If she's eating in, buzz her about halfway through her lunch hour and say, "As soon as you're free. . ." This will help her to realize the urgency of the day's tasks.

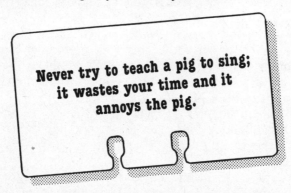

**11.** Pay no attention to complaints that she can't read your handwriting — your mother can read it, so it can't be all that bad. It's just that if you took the time to learn to write legibly, you wouldn't be where you are today.

**12.** Ask her to make photocopies of articles that interest you personally. She'll be impressed by your broad range of concerns.

# A STUDY OF SECRETARIES' CHANGING ATTITUDES, 1981 vs. 1972

To what extent do you agree — or disagree — with the following statements?

| | Agree Strongly | | Moderately Agree | | Moderately Disagree | | Stongly Disagree | | Not Sure | |
|---|---|---|---|---|---|---|---|---|---|---|
| | 1981 | 1972 | 1981 | 1972 | 1981 | 1972 | 1981 | 1972 | 1981 | 1972 |
| a) Secretaries should put loyalty to their bosses ahead of loyalty to the organization. | 8% | 18% | 47% | 34% | 27% | 24% | 12% | 13% | 6% | 6% |
| b) A good secretary is willing to do personal chores for the boss. | 11% | 58% | 51% | 36% | 17% | 36% | 16% | 3% | 5% | 1% |
| c) Secretaries should sacrifice their own job satisfaction, if necessary, to help their bosses accomplish their work | 10% | 43% | 28% | 34% | 34% | 12% | 24% | 6% | 4% | 2% |
| d) A secretary has the right to refuse to do personal chores for the boss' family. | 62% | 20% | 23% | 34% | 10% | 23% | 3% | 15% | 2% | 4% |
| e) Secretaries should put their own welfare and advancement ahead of that of the boss. | 12% | 4% | 34% | 13% | 31% | 26% | 13% | 46% | 10% | 5% |
| f) Secretarial salaries are not comparable to the work and responsibilities the job includes. | 57% | n.a. | 29% | n.a. | 7% | n.a. | 4% | n.a. | 0% | n.a. |
| g) Working for a woman is not as pleasant as working for a man. | 22% | 44% | 16% | 21% | 19% | 10% | 21% | 7% | 22% | 13% |
| k) Secretaries are more respected today than they were five years ago. | 27% | n.a. | 49% | n.a. | 11% | n.a. | 6% | n.a. | 7% | n.a. |
| i) Working women are more respected today than they were five years ago. | 43% | n.a. | 48% | n.a. | 5% | n.a. | 2% | n.a. | 2% | n.a. |

n.a. — not asked

Source: Special Report: Secretaries Tell What They Think, What They Want (1981). Reprinted with permission and copyrighted by The Research Institute of America, Inc.

**13.** When she's trying to meet a deadline, don't offer to pick up your own phone calls. It might set a dangerous precedent.

**14.** Don't hesitate to have your spouse and children ask her to do their personal typing. It promotes that "one big happy family" feeling.

**15.** Ignore her hints that her salary is not keeping up with inflation. After all, how can you stay abreast of inflation if the people on the lower levels keep getting more money?

**16.** Do a lot of silent pondering while she's in your office with her shorthand book. The long pauses will give her time to admire the depth of your thinking.

**17.** Insist that she help out the other secretaries when they fall behind. She'll enjoy the camaraderie of the steno pool.

**18.** When she calls in sick, make her realize how much it inconveniences you. This will encourage her not to malinger.

**19.** Leave that all-important letter until 4:52 P.M. Don't mention it ahead of time, though, or she'll think up some reason why she has to leave at 5:00.

**20.** When she hands in her resignation, don't waste time on introspection. Remember that many secretaries are just plain capricious. As Freud once said so perceptively, "What do these women want?"

---

**THE SIX STAGES OF ALL PROJECTS**
1. Wild Enthusiasm
2. Disillusionment
3. Total Confusion
4. Search for the Guilty
5. Punishment of the Innocent
6. Promotion of the Non-Participants

---

The twenty ways to please your secretary is taken from an article "How to Please Your Secretary" by Miranda Morse. It is © 1980 by The New York Times Company and reprinted by permission.

CHAPTER

# 16

# WARNING: SECRETARIAL WORK CAN BE HAZARDOUS TO YOUR HEALTH

## INTRODUCTION

Office work, once considered safe, clean work, is now known to involve serious health hazards.

The past two years have seen an explosion of concern among health experts — and among office workers themselves.

Concern over *industrial* health and safety goes back many years. Government standards and union contracts have provided safeguards against some of these hazards.

The full extent of the dangers of office work is not yet known. Yet scientific studies have now firmly established that health and safety hazards for office workers are serious and widespread. Constant sitting in poorly designed chairs, "stuffy" office air polluted by irritating fumes, a stressful work pace and tight deadlines — these were once accepted as "just part of the job." Now these working conditions are recognized as potential hazards to office workers' health.

AUTHOR'S NOTE: Most of this book is written in a light-hearted way that is meant to entertain as well as educate. This chapter however is a serious look at a serious subject. It is an abridged version of a study entitled WARNING: HEALTH HAZARDS FOR OFFICE WORKERS. The study was prepared by the Working Women Education Fund in 1981. Anyone interested in obtaining a copy of the complete study of this most important topic should send a check for $5 to 9 to 5, 1225 Huron Rd., Cleveland, Ohio 44115.

As the economy has changed, clerical workers have replaced manufacturing workers as the single largest sector of the workforce. More than half of all new jobs will be white collar in the 1980s. Some business spokesmen predict that by the year 2029, 80 to 90% of the entire workforce will be in jobs involving information processing. This shift has heightened interest in office working conditions.

Research indicates that the hazards of office work have a particular impact on women, who are most likely to occupy the most highly regimented jobs, experience the greatest stress, and have the heaviest home responsibilities on top of their job duties.

We now know that it's not only the highly paid executive who is likely to get a heart attack from the heavy responsibilities of his job. It's also his secretary! In fact, an unsupportive boss may be hazardous to your health.

# OVERWORKED AND UNDERPAID

Office job hazards appear to be worsening. The rapid rise in office automation is maximizing the factors that can lead to stress-related disease — such as machines that cause muscle strain, long hours of sitting, repetitive tasks, low control over work pace, and shift work. Today, 22% of all office machine operators work evening or night shifts, compared to 10% of all white collar workers.

The drive for energy conservation has led to "sealing" of older buildings and construction of "tight" new offices. Poorly maintained humidification systems can allow infectious bacteria to breed. Inadequate ventilation can recycle bacteria, dust, cigarette smoke, and harmful airborne chemicals throughout the building. In this sealed environment, the increased use of synthetic furnishings and supplies and machines that emit toxic fumes can turn offices into "virtual gas chambers." In addition, many clericals work in proximity to industrial plants where they may be exposed to industrial fumes, high noise levels, and other problems.

## JOB STRESS IN THE OFFICE

### A STRESS EPIDEMIC

Recent research is beginning to uncover a virtual epidemic of stress symptoms and stress-related disease among office workers. Millions of workers are affected. And because the symptoms do not end when the worker walks out of the office at the end of a day's work, the families of millions may also be affected by the problems caused by office job stress.

Furthermore, the trend toward automation in office work is exacerbating the very job factors found to be most stressful, while threatening to eliminate those aspects of the job which promote job satisfaction and counteract stress.

Within the last year, the public and the scientific community have been shocked into recognizing the high levels of job stress endured by women office workers.

* Results from the Framingham Heart Study (February, 1980) showed that women clerical and secretarial workers developed coronary heart disease (CHD)—clearly identified as a stress-related malady—at nearly twice the rate of other women workers.

* The National Institute of Occupational Safety and Health (NIOSH), studying the insurance office of Blue Shield in San Francisco, found higher levels of job stress among operators of video display terminals (VDTs) in strictly clerical jobs than *any other* occupational group ever studied by NIOSH—including air traffic controllers.

Surely stress has been part of office work for a very long time. But, today stress and its effects on health command increasing attention. Why? For one thing, the major causes of death in the U.S. have changed over the last century from infectious diseases to chronic killers such as cancer and CHD. Through research, scientists can demonstrate the role of a lifetime's exposure to stress at work in these diseases and many more. This formerly "unseen" or "hidden" hazard is coming into focus.

The new findings about stress among office workers came as a surprise; they are still met with resistant disbelief by many managers. One fact which helps to account for some of the surprise; before the 1970's, virtually all stress research was done with white men only. Women workers were not included in most studies. To this day, there is almost no research on job stress experienced by minority workers. Among white-collar workers, "executive stress" or "managerial stress" received a great deal of attention, while clerical and secretarial workers were ignored until recently.

The combined roles of paid work and work at home for women, and the prevalence of hypertension among the black population are examples of "complicating factors" which led researchers to exclude these workers from previous studies. Now, these same factors lead many researchers to predict that they will find more harmful health effects from stress than were measured among managers or young, white male workers. In particular, race discrimination may act as a constant, underlying source of stress, adding a daily dose of hostility or isolation, or both, to each workday.

## STRESS IN THE OFFICE

A study by the National Institute of Occupational Safety and Health (NIOSH) conducted in 1975 found that secretaries had the second highest incidence of stress-related diseases among 22,000 workers in 130 occupations. The research team identified 1) rapid work-pacing, especially machine-pacing, 2) long working hours and 3) repetitive or monotonous work as the factors leading to high levels of stress among very different jobs. (Secretaries ranked second after unskilled laborers.)

Results of the Framingham Heart Study released in February, 1980 show that women clerical workers developed coronary heart disease (CHD) — clearly identified as a stress-related disease — at almost twice the rate of other women workers including housewives (previously thought to be a greater risk than working women). Furthermore the 8-year study found that women clerical workers with children and blue-collar husbands developed CHD at nearly twice the rate of all *men* workers.

## KEY SOURCES OF JOB STRESS

Previous research identifies major causes of stress which affect employees in vastly different jobs:

**Heavy Workload.** Too much work to do in too little time comes up again and again as one of the top sources of stress. In studies of air traffic controllers, the men in the areas of the most dense traffic were the ones who developed hypertension at a very early age, while controllers in areas of normal traffic flow showed an average incidence of the health problem.

Insufficient staffing and unreasonably high demands for "output" are frequent problems for office workers. Conflicting demands from "too many bosses" often compounds the stressfulness of a heavy workload. Balance is very important in workload problems, as researchers point out that *too little* work can also cause stress. The "quality" of the workload should be considered, too. An especially bad combination is having too much work (a "quantitative overload") which holds too little interest or offers too little challenge (a "qualitative underload"). Such a combination becomes even more common with the advent of automation in lower-level office jobs.

**Long Working Hours.** Previous studies of male workers provide evidence of a strong relationship between long working hours and stress-related disease. One study found that men who worked 48 hours a week in light industry had twice the rate of death from coronary heart disease as those who did the same work for no more than 40 hours a week. Secretaries and clericals in certain jobs cite frequent unexpected overtime, usually mandatory, to meet deadlines or handle seasonable heavy volumes of work.

Some researchers believe that overtime and heavy workload are only significant when correlated with job satisfaction. In other words, when a person is *rewarded* for extra time and effort, his or her health is *not* as likely to be adversely affected as that of someone in a dead-end job, according to the results of recent studies.

PAST DUE

**Rapid Pacing and Machine Pacing of Work** are very powerful factors in stress-related symptoms. NIOSH researchers believe that rapid work pace is one of the major reasons for their findings of extremely high levels of job stress among secretarial and clerical workers.

Office work has traditionally involved meeting many deadlines, making fast, frequent decisions, and carrying out quick transactions. Today, office work is being "speeded-up" as factory-based methods of time-motion study are being applied inappropriately to information-processing work.

Recent years have seen an increase in the use of automatic call distributors, prompters, production quotas and computerized monitoring of clerical work. Management introduces these devices in efforts to "increase productivity" by taking control over the speed of work away from the office workers themselves. But research is beginning to show that performance often declines along with job satisfaction when control over work pace is transferred from people to machines or computers. In studies of machine-paced vs. self-paced work, error rates increase from 40 to 400%.

**Monotonous/Repetitive Work.** Studies find the highest rates of total fatigue of exhaustion associated with the highest reports of monotony on the job. Monotonous work which requires close attention to detail but holds little interest for the employee is particularly stressful. Doing the same stereotyped motion all day causes muscular fatigue as well as job dissatisfaction. Performing the same set of routines without the chance to learn new skills can lead to boredom, frustration and decline in self-esteem.

**Service Work.** There are special pressures in jobs which involve responsibility for people (rather than things), notably in the health and medical industries and in social services employment.

Customer service representatives for banks, utilities, public agencies and insurance companies are in constant contact with clients, frequently handling complaints. Women office workers rarely have the authority to make decisions which could solve the problem. Bureaucratic procedures and rigid production quotas are often imposed.

**Discrimination as an "Institutional stressor."** The cumulative effect of experiencing discrimination on the basis of sex, race, age or combinations of the three, amounts to chronic stress for many women office workers. Such discrimination manifests itself on a personal level, on an institutional basis — in long-term denial of promotions and training, and in crisis events such as being fired, threatened with dismissal or urged to take early retirement.

**Lack of Recognition/Lack of Respect.** Women office workers suffer from a lack of recognition for their contribution to the overall effort, as well as from low pay and unfair treatment. Clerical workers frequently complain that they are "treated like children" or "treated like machines," and rarely granted their due measure of respect.

**Strategies for Reducing Stress.** Because workplaces and individuals vary, it's important to identify the sources of stress at play in a *particular* job, department or company. However, some common strategies for reducing job stress for office workers can be described:

- **Environmental.** Reduce noise, improve ventilation and lighting, remove toxic chemicals from use, provide a lounge area for rest and social interaction.
- **Job Design.** Redesign jobs to allow more variety, provide adequate rest periods and job rotation, opportunities to learn

new skills, increased job decision latitude, increased control over workload and pace, realistic production standards.

- **Employer/Employee Relations.** Change the style of supervision and train supervisors in human relations, provide respect, recognition and effective grievance procedures, implement fair and non-discriminatory promotion and salary policies, increase workers' participation in decision making.
- **Socio-Economic.** Include mental health counselling coverage in benefit package, make accommodations to the needs of the working family — such as flex-time and child care, support continuing education provide access to advancement and training opportunities, improve pay and benefits, increase job security.

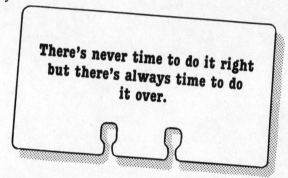

There's never time to do it right but there's always time to do it over.

Methods of stress reduction may require organizational representation, and/or assistance in organizational efforts, among clericals. Because most office workers generally do not have unions, less formal support groups are a necessary route to reducing stress. Assertiveness training, organizing skills, assistance in approaching and "negotiating" with management are all skills which office workers will need to make changes in their work environment. Many unions have formed special committees or task forces to address stress as part of their health and safety activity.

In summary, the role of chronic job stress in physical illness and psychological strain is very complex. Physical and emotional responses to stress are not neatly separable but build on one another. Although it is not possible to say exactly how particular stressors on the job lead to particular health problems, there is enough evidence to guide us in figuring out strategies to reduce and eliminate stress from women office workers' jobs. The research findings that we already have make it clear that steps to eliminate stress in the office need to be taken now, even while more research is underway.

**Modern offices are full of little conveniences.**

**Watch out.**

Office work can be hazardous to your health. Watch out for:

☐ Poor air quality and ventilation.
☐ Fumes from photocopiers.
☐ Toxic substances in solvents and toners.
☐ Excessive noise.
☐ Poor lighting or glare.
☐ Inadequate rest areas.
☐ Problems with video display terminals and other machines.
☐ Excessive job stress.
☐ Accidents due to poor office design or crowding.

Then, call WORKING WOMEN for help. We're organizing for fair pay, equal employment, respect . . . and a safe and healthy office.

**216/566-9308**

Working Women
1224 Huron Road
Cleveland, OH 44115
216/566-9308

CORRECTION FLUID

18 mL

Lenora Davis Design/Chicago

14" x 21" Glossy Poster also available from **Working Women.**
$3.00 each   $25 for 10   $60 for 25

# VIDEO DISPLAY TERMINALS

By 1985, more than ten million people will use video display terminals (VDTs) at work. Observers estimate that a new VDT is installed every thirteen minutes, and experts predict that 10% of all workplaces will have at least one display unit in the near future. They are already used extensively in banks, insurance companies, law firms—in any industry where large secretarial pools are employed.

In 1979-80, the NIOSH conducted a study of video display terminal operators at the request of a coalition of labor unions. Five worksites were examined, including newspaper offices and the clerical departments of Blue Shield in San Francisco. Eighty to ninety percent of the clerical VDT operators experienced eye strain or muscle strain. High levels of anxiety, depression and fatigue were reported by VDT users at all of the worksites.

The NIOSH research team found that VDT operators in strictly clerical type operations showed *higher stress ratings than any group of workers NIOSH has ever studied including air traffic controllers.*

Clerical workers using VDTs were compared with a "control group" consisting of office clericals doing similar work but with pen and paper, conventional typewriters, and with professionals using terminals—mainly newspaper reporters and editors. All of the clericals reported high levels of anxiety, confusion, depression and fatigue, as well as very high rates of physical health problems. The "VDT clericals" experienced the highest levels of job stress, while the "VDT professionals" had reported the lowest stress levels with the "control clericals" in the middle. A vivid description of the differences in working conditions for the clericals and professional follows:

"When the job features of the various groups are examined we see that the clerical VDT operators held jobs involving rigid work procedures with high production standards, constant pressure for performance, very little operator control over job tasks, and little identification with and satisfaction from the end product of their work activity. In contrast to the clerical VDT operators, the professionals using VDTs held jobs that allowed for flexibility, control over job tasks, utilization of their education and a great deal of satisfaction and pride in their end product. While both jobs had tight deadline requirements, the professional operators had a great deal of control over how these would be met. In their case, the VDT was a tool that could be used for enhancing their end product, while for the clerical VDT operators, the VDT was part of a new technology that took more and more meaning out of their work. It's not surprising that the professionals using VDTs did not report levels of job stress as high as the clerical VDT operators. . .This suggests that the use of the VDT is not the only factor contributing to operator stress levels health complaints, but that job content also makes a contribution."

## HEALTH SYMPTOMS RELATED TO VDT USE

Conclusive information on the long-term effects of VDT use will take years to obtain and analyze, but the short-term effects are already well documented even though the causal mechanisms are not yet understood: eyestrain; headache; short-term loss of visual acuity and changes in color perception; back, neck and shoulder pain; fatigue; stomach aches and vomiting.

Health symptoms may result from problems in machine, workstation, office environment or job design, or a combination of these. Eyestrain is often worse for employees doing "terminal intensive" work—looking at an "interactive" terminal all day or looking back and forth between hard copy and a screen continuously. Muscular strain in the neck, shoulder, back, hands and wrists is often worse for data entry workers who do not look at the screen as often, but must adopt awkward set postures to work at top speed for hours on end.

Eyestrain, postural problems and musculo-skeletal problems are aggravated by poor lighting, uncomfortable chairs, mismatched chair, desk and keyboard heights, lack of workspace, humidity, temperature and air quality problems, bright, shiny surrounding walls and surfaces which maximize glare, and a general lack of adjustability afforded the office worker(s) using VDTs. When an office worker's chair, keyboard and screen, and lighting are all unadjustable, it is she who must do all the adjusting. The result: a set of problems which compounds the stressfullness of the job and threatens one's health.

**Machine Problems.** Although improved equipment is available, there are still a great many low quality models on the market and in use. Frequent problems with machine design include: "nauseating colors" especially fluorescent green, "low resolution" images which lack contrast from background color or generally lack clarity; characters that are too small, too faint or otherwise difficult to read; overly flickering images due to an inadequate "refresh rate" in cheap machines or inadequate maintenance and replacement of cathode ray tubes; shiny keys and casings designed to look "space-like" without regard for the excess glare they cause the user; keyboards attached to screens which can't be adjusted for viewing distance or angle. Since anti-reflection filters are optional components for purchase, they are too often overlooked in the name of office economy.

**Lighting problems** are probably the biggest complaints from display screen users. Work at VDTs is very demanding visually, much more so than reading newsprint or a book for the same amount of time. One study found that under laboratory conditions, 50% of the subjects reported a burning sensation in the eyes, 33% reported headaches, and 25% experienced flickering vision. The study found that the operators experienced a 50% deterioration in visual clarity, especially severe after four hours of uninterrupted use.

The problems caused by VDT work are increased by lighting conditions designed for traditional office work, according to Swedish scientist Dr. Olav Ostberg. Ostberg estimates that typical office lighting will cause discomfort for about half of all VDT users. Office workers often find that they need to wear tinted glasses to reduce glare. A combination of more subdued overhead lighting and adjustable "spot-lighting" for copy or "input" is helpful, but not always readily provided.

**Workstation design.** As much flexibility as possible should be provided. Work spaces should not be overcrowded so that build-ups of heat, noise or stuffy air are avoided. Chairs and desks should be adjustable since office workers themselves come in all different heights.

**Office Environment.** Altogether, office environments reflect too little attention to the comfort of the office workers who must sit in them all day. Appearance and fancy new equipment is unfortunately more important to some managers than their employees' state of health.

**Visual Strain.** A recent study in Vienna found that clarity of visual focus did not return to normal for more than 16 minutes after four hours of work at a display screen, even with a 15 minute break. The Viennese government therefore proposed a limit of four hours of work at a screen per day with a 15 minute break after two hours. The vision of terminal operators undergoes short-term changes described as "minor" by the U.S. NIOSH. But the agency expresses concern that these temporary changes may indicate "the potential for chronic effects given long-term CRT use." An industrial hygienist warns that VDTs "exaggerate the deficiencies in vision or any defects in the eyes."

**Low-level Radiation Emissions**. The original health concerns of workers on video display terminals had to do with the issue of radiation. Early NIOSH studies looked at the cataractogenic potential of VDTs, finding that radiation emissions by VDTs were below federal threshold standards.

A grievance filed by the Newspaper Guild prompted a 1977 study by NIOSH of the potential radiation dangers of VDTs. Two newspaper employees who had worked continuously on VDTs developed bilateral, posterior cataracts (the type caused by radiant energy exposure). Most regions of the electromagnetic spectrum have been implicated as being cataractogenic. Although NIOSH found that all categories of radiation emission by VDT's were below threshold standards, the etiology of the employees' cataracts remained undetermined. The type of cataract observed has only four known causes; neither man had any medical history pointing to the other three causes.

## HEALTH STANDARDS FOR VDTs/CRTs

An excellent readable guide to proper lighting standards, workstation design, and criteria of high-quality equipment is available from the New York Committee for Occupational Safety and Health, called **Health Protection for Operators of VDTs/CRTs**. Important points about machine and workstation design include:

Screens should be detached from keyboards so they are adjustable.
Screens, keyboards, and room decor should be in mat, subdued colors to reduce glare; conventional office lighting should be redesigned.
Look for "high resolution" screens, proper size, color and clarity of screen characters.
Screens should allow individual operators to adjust angle, brightness and focus for viewing comfort.
Too often, devices which reduce glare and/or noise are optional — make sure they are purchased.
Regular maintenance and repair are essential.

Only high quality equipment should be used, and flexibility should be built into programming and systems design. Automation in the office has the potential to reduce rather than increase stress if the following job design principles are followed:

New technology should mean you use more skills in your work, not fewer, and that promotional opportunities are increased, not reduced.

New office technology should mean more control over the pace and organization of work, not less control.

Increased productivity should be compensated by increased pay, more breaktime, and/or a reduction in weekly hours without a reduction in pay.

Adequate rest periods and job rotation are the key to protecting the health and well-being of video-display terminal operators. The NIOSH recommends a 15-minute break per hour of visually intensive work and 15 minutes per two hours of continuous work at a VDT to reduce eyestrain and stress. In other countries, limits of one and a half hours continuous VDT work and/or four hours per day have been recommended or mandated.

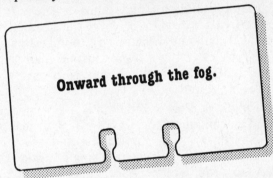

## OFFICE AIR QUALITY AND VENTILATION PROBLEMS

"We always thought people got 'Monday morning sickness' because they didn't like coming back to work. Now we're realizing that it may be because they're coming into an environment that's an irritation to their system," explains Craig Hollowell, Director of Indoor Air Quality Program at the Lawrence Berkeley Laboratories.

Energy conservation, new building and furniture materials (particularly plastic-based synthetics in furnishings and either chemical or paper-based insulation materials), office supplies and machines which emit fumes, the "weatherless" office with its sealed windows, and improperly maintained or faulty ventilation systems that can recycle infectious bacteria, dust, smoke and harmful airborne chemical contaminants throughout a building — all of these factors are causing an explosion of concern about office air quality. "There's probably more damage to human health by indoor pollution than by outdoor pollution," says a scientist for the World Health Organization.

The effects of poor office air quality range from fatigue, lethargy, headaches, and mucous membrane irritation or skin rashes, to nausea, colds, bronchitis, increased stress and menstrual irregularities, to long-term respiratory diseases. Some airborne toxic substances, such as asbestos or ozone can lead to blood diseases, or possible mutagenic damage or cancer. Many others, such as methanol and organic solvents, can cause "a drunken state," blurred vision or nervous conditions.

So many outbreaks of building-related health problems have occurred in the past few years that scientists coined the term "Tight Building Syndrome" to describe these "mystery illnesses." Perhaps as many as 30% of all requests for on-site health evaluations received by the NIOSH last year involved office workers. In only a few cases has the agency been able to find a chemical "cause," but faulty ventilation plays a major role as does stress. Employees have been forced to recognize the dangers of poor air quality in "sealed" buildings because large numbers of employees have become too sick or too drowsy to work, many have called in public health officials, and some employees have walked out of their offices in protest.

**"Sealed" Buildings.** Poor ventilation is a key environmental contributor to air contamination. Office machines such as photocopiers, specialized printing, duplicating and new "signature-writing" machines are often located in small, windowless rooms or in closets to reduce office noise. This only increases the dangers of accumulating toxic concentrations of byproducts such as ozone, methanol, formaldehyde and aromatic hydrocarbons. If the exhaust flows into an air-conditioning system rather than to the outside, the air contaminants can be recycled through the entire work area.

"Sealed" older buildings and newly constructed "energy-efficient" buildings pose more problems for office workers. An inadequate supply of fresh air means that the percentage of oxygen in the office air declines. Lack of fresh air can produce headaches, make one drowsy or faint, and can interfere with concentration.

Air exchange rates of 15 to 20 complete changeovers of fresh air per working day are recommended. Dr. Hollowell of Berkeley Laboratories found that "a new energy-efficient structure typically allows **but one air exchange every 10 hours.**" In buildings where smoking is permitted, five times as much ventilation is required to remove the soot, carbon monoxide and benzopyrene released. NIOSH researchers have found that increasing air exchange rates per day goes a long way toward relieving symptoms.

By closing off exhaust ventilation and cutting down the movement of air inside, the indoor equivalent of "smog" is born. Air refresheners, solvents, adhesives in building products, cleaning fluids, fire-retardant chemicals, chemicals which prevent aging of paints and finishes — all these are trapped inside. "We may be transforming offices into virtual gas chambers," says Dr. George Burch of Tulane University Medical School.

Ventilation and air quality are often worst around clerical workspaces, since clerical workers are usually located farthest from windows, even when a window can be opened. And, in most cases, they are closest to and spend the most time using office machines which emit fumes.

**Temperature and Humidity Problems**. Allergic reactions, fatigue, colds, respiratory problems, dry skin, and general discomfort can result from poor humidity and temperature controls. Too much or too little humidity can compound eye irritation from pollutants, adding to the strain of intense visual work. The effects are often worse for wearers of contact lenses.

**Organic Pollutants**. The classic case of health effects involving biological agents indoors was the Legionnaire's Disease in a hotel in Philadelphia. Now several other organisms and allergies have been identified and associated with workers in offices.

**Hypersensitivity pneumonitis** — also called "humidifier lung" may appear to be flu, but is caused by bacterial infection. Primary sources of these organisms are cooling towers or evaporative condensers and humidifier reservoirs.

Scientists who investigated a large office complex of 4,000 employees found 50 cases of hypersensitivity pneumonitis. They estimate that such infections happen often, affecting from 3 to 16% of those exposed in a given office. These risks are increased in large-space offices with forced-air circulation systems. Insulation material based on organic compounds such as newsprint can also provide breeding grounds for bacteria and spores.

**Toxic Contaminants in Office Air**. Sources of office air contaminants include exhaust fumes of office machines and special printing processes, vapors from common office products, nearby laboratories or industrial processes, outdoor pollutants drawn inside and asbestos fibers loosened from insulation in older buildings. There are more than 20 possible airborne irritants under study in relation to office workers' health complaints.

Several guides are available which provide information on symptoms, effects, legal limits of exposure, and levels of exposure which cause health symptoms. A few of the most prevalent and potentially dangerous toxic hazards in offices are described below.

COPY

**Photocopiers**. There are at least four types of hazards associated with photocopying machines: 1) **ozone** in exhaust emissions; 2) dangerous chemicals in toners such as **nitropyrene**; 3) chemicals used in the photocopying **process**, such as **trinitrofluorenone**; and 4) potential exposure to **ultra-violet radiant light**.

Photocopiers should be in well-ventilated areas. If necessary local exhaust vents should be installed near machines to remove fumes to the outside. Machines should be regularly cleaned and maintained, and ozone levels should be measured and kept below the Occupational Safety and Health Administration (OSHA) limit. Clerical workers should know what chemicals are in toners and make sure nitropyrene is not present.

**Chemicals in Office Products.** Other potentially harmful chemicals contained in commonly used office supplies include: **trichloroethylene** (TCE), **tetrachloroethylene perchloroethylene**, both suspected carcinogens found in liquid eraser products; **benzene**, a carcinogen, and **toluene**, a powerful narcotic, found as impurities in cleaning solvents. At moderate levels of exposure to organic solvents workers complain of eye irritation, changes in skin color, and heart palpitations. Several deaths have been connected to the sniffing of a typewriter correction fluid.

Many common office products are also potential causal agents of skin rashes for clerical workers: adhesives, carbon or "carboness" paper, copy paper, duplicating fluids and materials, inks and ink removers, rubber, solvents, type-cleaner, and typewriter ribbons.

Since manufacturers of office products are not required to label them, other harmful chemicals may also be in use. It is crucial to obtain information on what solvents and substances are being used and determine their health effects and safe use. Requiring manufacturers to label product contents and requiring employers to post contents and instructions for safe use would be a positive first step.

**Airborne Asbestos**. Asbestos is a well-documented and severe health hazard. Exposure can cause: **asbestosis** (a chronic lung ailment); **cancer** of the lungs, esophagus, stomach, colon and rectum; and **mesothelioma**, an invariably fatal form of cancer involving the thin membrane lining of the chest and abdomen. The latency period between exposure and appearance of disease may be 20 to 40 years. **There is no safe level of exposure to asbestos fibers**. The particles are extremely durable and very difficult to destroy or degrade. Fibers remain airborn for long periods of time and are inhaled easily. Particles that are retained in the lungs stay indefinitely. Asbestos exposure at work also endangers the employee's family if particles are carried home on clothes. For cigarette smokers, exposure increases the likelihood of lung cancer 30 to 90 fold.

**Cigarette smoke** in the office environment is a further hazard to smokers and non-smokers alike. According to one environmental consultant, "The level of particulate matter in office buildings where smoking is allowed is 10 to 100 times higher than the allowable limits for outside air." For clerical workers who spend all day sitting, the effects of smoking on health are magnified, since carbon monoxide from cigarettes stays in the bloodstream longer during low physical activity. A recent epidemiological study concluded that long-term exposure to smoke, limited to work environment only (i.e.,not at home), is deleterious to the non-smoker and significantly reduces small-airway function to the same extent as smoking one to ten cigarettes per day." Cigarette smoke contains numerous potent carcinogens, including benzopyrene, affects not only the lungs but many other organs, and maximizes the effects of other indoor air pollutants because of the density and persistence of particulate matter released. In addition, many legal secretaries and clerks in law offices complain of cigar smoke. Preliminary experiments show that one cigar generates three times the respirable particles of the average cigarette and up to 30 times as much carbon monoxide. There is a great need for improved ventilation and creation of "non-smoking" areas to protect the two-thirds of U.S. adults who do not smoke.

**Tight Building Syndrome.** Typical symptoms of tight building syndrome include: fatigue and lethargy (even numbers of employees falling asleep at their desks at about the same time of day); headaches, nausea, dizziness, or lightheadedness, problems with vision, irritated nose and throat; difficulty breathing or asthma-like symptoms; frequent and widespread colds and sore throats; and menstrual irregularities (including intermittent spotting between periods, prolonged or continuous menstruation for weeks or even months, and missing menstrual periods). However there are many potential causes for such problems, and individuals should see a doctor for medical evaluation. Previously such problems were often deemed the result of "hysteria" on the part of workers, but tight building syndrome is now understood as a "disease entity" related to the work environment.

Researchers describe several types of factors known to bring about this set of health symptoms: 1) irritating and/or toxic indoor air pollutants; 2) biological agents such as fungi, spores, bacteria; 3) inadequate supply of fresh air, stagnant and/or very dry air; 4) high levels of job stress — excessive work demands, highly regimented work, and/or problems with supervisory style. There is usually a physical 'trigger,' a toxic or irritating air pollutant, but at too low a level to account for the widespread health symptoms.

## SUMMARY

Low levels of air contaminants, permissible under government standards, can still have adverse effects on health. People with allergies, respiratory or nervous system problems are often especially affected. Accidents become more likely if employees are drowsy, lightheaded, giddy or dizzy from inhaling fumes. High levels of job stress can increase the effects of low level exposures, while decreasing resistance to illness.

The combined effects of exposure to low levels of several chemicals at once are not well understood, nor are the effects of many years of exposure to very small doses of toxics well documented. For certain substances, scientists point out that no safe levels are known. New chemicals are introduced at such a rapid rate that harmful effects are only discovered many years later.

Furthermore, many allergy specialists are concerned that an increasing number of patients have become oversensitized to all materials made from petrochemicals and other synthetics — even perfumes and some man-made fabrics. Once damaged, the immune system (which should protect the body) reacts constantly and drastically, causing symptoms which include muscle pain, aches or spasms, extreme weakness, or breathing difficulty. Many of these patients are former office workers who have no known chemical over-exposure outside of their workplace.

New York State and the city of Philadelphia now have "Right-to-Know" laws which require employers and manufacturers to inform employees of the contents, possible health effects, and procedures for safe use of substances used in the workplace. The Philadelphia law also requires that doctors and public officials will be provided with lists of all potentially hazardous substances and associated symptoms. Other countries have laws to ensure improved indoor air quality and to protect employees against low level toxic exposures.

Some steps to improve office air quality include:

- Proper architectural and ventilation engineering design which ensures a good supply of fresh air, adequate air turnover rate, and ventilation of any toxic air pollutants to the outside.

- Offices should be "aired" periodically by opening windows (in off-hours during winter months). Inexpensive air and heat exchanges may prove useful.

- Regular maintenance of ventilation systems and machines is essential; logs should record cleaning, and repair schedules should be available to employees to bring attention to health problems.

- Allow employees some control over temperature, humidity and air flow controls, to protect themselves from extremes and drafts.

- Install or "unseal" windows; design buildings which allow the maximum number of employees access to windows which can be opened; don't sacrifice windows in renovating older buildings.

- Special care should be taken to provide exhaust ventilation in workrooms or any areas where printing and copying machines are used; improved filtration methods are needed.

- Substitute safe products for those containing toxic substances; write to manufacturers for "Material (or Product) Safety Data Sheets" on their products and post contents and instructions for safe use.

- If potentially dangerous materials must be handled as part of a job, wear protective gloves and avoid inhalation.

- Jobs should be designed to involve a variety of tasks, so that no one does photocopying or duplicating excessively, for example.

- Airborne asbestos fibers should be immediately eliminated; well-established safety procedures should be followed if asbestos insulation is repaired; if exposed, insulation should be sealed at once.

## DESIGN PROBLEMS IN THE OFFICE ENVIRONMENT

### Constant Sitting and Keyboard Work

Most women office workers use machines with keyboards typewriters, key entry machines, accounting machines, VDTs—for a substantial part of the day. They are particularly vulnerable to a variety of musculo-skeletal problems.

A survey of the scientific literature on the ergonomics of office work-related stress, prepared for NIOSH in 1979, reveals that 25% of the operators of keyboards (such as typewriters, keypunch, accounting machines and video-display terminals) studied were diagnosed as suffering from occupational cervico-brachial syndrome (OCBS), also referred to as occupational cramp-myalgia. About 50% of the office keyboard operators complained of muscular distress in the arm, neck and shoulders — symptomatic of OCBS. These problems are substantially worse for users of video-display terminals (VDTs), and are exacerbated by rapid work-pacing which is characteristic of clerical work.

Some scientists believe that static load production resulting from the dynamic muscular activity of the fingers while the muscles of the upper body operate statically in order to keep the hand properly positioned is inherent in conventional keyboard design. But excessive muscle strain can be dramatically *reduced* if ergonomic recommendations are followed in workplace design. Japanese scientists who observed office workers engaged in mechanical tasks recommended periodic examination, and emphasized job rotation and rest periods for such workers. The NIOSH literature review concludes that the importance of rest periods "cannot be over-emphasized."

Office workers are also particularly susceptible to musculo-skeletal problems, such as *tendonitis, carpal tunnel syndrome* and *tenosynovitis*, a painful inflammation of the tendons of the wrist due to overexertion from constant repetition of stereotyped movements. In additon to these problems, a Swedish study conducted in 1976 found that frequent *upper back pain* tends to accompany office computerization.

### Office Chairs

"Executives get the best chairs, and secretaries get the worst, which is too bad, because secretaries spend more time in them," remarks a University of Wisconsin professor who designed "model" chairs. Sitting all day can add to blood circulation problems, varicose veins, and hemorrhoids. Poorly designed office chairs and constant sitting contribute to muscle and spinal column tension, leading to *lower back pain* commonly cited by office workers, and can even lead to spinal damage. Again, rests from constant sitting and job rotation can reduce such health problems, although long-term solutions require job redesign and proper office furniture design standards such as other countries have. The least a manager can do for the clerical and secretarial staff in an office is to to buy each a good $75 or $90 chair, as many occupational health researchers recommend. From a cost-benefit point of view, a good chair pays for itself almost immediately in the time it saves the employees from "squiggling" and awkward motions and gestures in a non-adjustable chair. Dr. E.R. Tichauer of N.Y.U. estimates a gain of 40 minutes of productive working time per day when employees are provided with properly designed seating, which adds up to 21 working days a year. In one instance, an industrial engineer recommended an additional two hours per day for VDT users in the workplace studied to complete their work unless the uncomfortable, inflexible low quality chairs were replaced with well-designed ones.

## Lighting and Eye Strain

Many office workers work in areas where lighting is described as "twilight," while others suffer from glare, as offices often register a glare index of 24 rather than the recommended value of 19.9. Poor lighting often combines with other design problems.

## Noise

Experiments have shown that workers exposed to moderate or intense noise on the job have increased incidence of circulatory, digestive, neurological and psychiatric problems. Noise is also a major contributor to occupational stress for women office workers, and can cause fatigue. Prolonged exposure to noise levels above 90 dB(A), the OSHA limit, leads to hearing loss. Many scientists believe exposure at or below 85 dB can cause hearing problems.

Office noise levels are considered acceptable in the range of 55 to 70 dB. Typical *measured* levels of noise in offices with five machines operating register 64 to 73 dB(A), beyond recommended standards. Under such conditions, phone conversation is difficult and a normal voice can only be heard within a 2-foot range.

Typewriter noise is generally 63 to 69 decibels, while an office tabulating machine has a decibel level of 80 or above. An employee who works continuously on machines such as these in a small, confined room (as is often the case) encounters a potentially hazardous noise level. Years of noise exposure on the job have caused some keypunchers to suffer permanent partial hearing loss.

The illusion that large-space open offices solve the problem of noise is disproven by an ergonomic investigation of fifteen such offices in Switzerland. Noise levels still ranged from 56 to 64 decibels with machines operating. The upper limits cause stress and are considered loud enough to make phone and voice communication difficult and interfere with concentration.

Office noise can be absorbed by carpeting and plants, and reduced by mats under typewriters and plastic covers over typewriters and other equipment. But a better solution would be the production of "quiet" office machines. A typewriter manufacturer testified at a noise hearing that sound-attenuating materials could be built into electric typewriters at an additional manufacturing cost of only 60¢ per machine.

## OFFICE SAFETY HAZARDS

**Accidents and Injuries.** The U.S. Department of Labor estimates an annual rate of 40,000 disabling accidents among the nation's office workers, and approximately 200 office-related deaths per year. The most frequent causes are falls or slips, accounting for 50% of all office accidents; 20% of falls in one study were attributed to "chair design." Other frequent causes are lifting stress, and accidents which involve unstable file cabinets and shelving (generally striking against or being struck by objects). Accidents are most likely to occur during or just after an office move, and during office "rush hour" when a deadline must be met.

**Fire Hazards.** Concern over fire dangers in giant office complexes has been heightened by the tragic hotel fires of 1980. A number of factors increase the risks in modern offices. "The completely undivided ceiling" and floor-to-ceiling windows typical of large open-space offices make it possible for "an instantaneous flash of fire" to spread. Modern high-rises are "criss-crossed with wiring that may become overloaded." The widespread use of synthetic materials in buildings poses perhaps the most frightening new problems. When plastics burn, most generate fumes with poison gases. Dr. Jeanne Stellman writes that many fire deaths attributed to smoke inhalation are more accurately described "as due to chemical-fume poisoning." Lax enforcement of building and safety codes, codes inadequate to deal with modern fire dangers, and codes compromised for the sake of "economic development" at the cost of employees' safety only add further risks.

## CONCLUSION: A CALL FOR ACTION

Toxic chemicals, noise, inadequate lighting, poor equipment design, and accidents pose serious health hazards for millions of office workers. Stressful pace, job design, low pay, and other working conditions cause a further strain on office workers. As a result, office workers are particularly prone to job-stress-related diseases.

As the office workforce grows, these dangers must be addressed. Office health hazards can and must be reduced. Manufacturers, employers, employees, and government must take immediate action toward office worker safety and health.

The drive for high corporate profits is no justification for the destruction of office workers' health and well-being. Yet even those who could sacrifice employee health for higher profits must recognize that the small savings achieved by skimping on noise control devices or fresh air supply may well represent false economy. Productivity suffers and absenteeism rises when working conditions take a toll on employees' health. Efficiency and accuracy decline along with job satisfaction when demands for speed and produciton are too high. Workers' Compensation for on-the-job-stress is granted only after the damage is already done. Preventive measures are needed to protect office workers' lives on the job.

Many office health hazards can be simply and inexpensively reduced:

*Stress reduction* can be achieved by changing the supervision style, redesigning jobs to allow for more variety and recognition, creating advancement and training opportunities, and providing adequate rest breaks. Accommodation to the needs of the working family — e.g., flex-time and child care — can also reduce stress for many employees.

Some relief from the risks associated with *video-display terminals* can result from frequent rest breaks, improved adjustable machinery, and maximum flexibility and comfort in workstation design. Jobs involving VDT work should allow greater control over the pace and organization of work. Job redesign may be required to reduce stress and improve job satisfaction.

Problems associated with *sitting at a keyboard* for long periods can be minimized by better chair and equipment design, rest breaks, and rotation of tasks.

Noise can be reduced by the introduction of sound-absorbent materials into the office, by modifications of office machines and by the manufacture of quieter machines. Adjustable lighting and materials that reduce glare can relieve visual strain.

Inexpensive modifications in *ventilation* systems can keep fuel costs down while also improving air quality. Regular cleaning and maintenance is a must.

Exposure to some *toxic chemicals* may exceed government limits. Lower-level exposures, within legal guidelines, can still have adverse health effects. Adequate exhaust ventilation and the substitution of safer products can help to eliminate these hazards. For chemicals where standards do not yet exist or safe levels are not yet known, a cautious approach that protects employees from exposure—before it is too late—is essential.

*Accidents and injuries* can be prevented through proper equipment, better training, and planning to avoid unnecessary rush periods. The dangers of *fires* in the office buildings have increased. Fire precautions need urgent attention and improvement.

## Manufacturers

Manufacturers must act responsibly to minimize the health hazards in office products and machines. In many cases, pressure from European unions and buyers has led to the development of safer technology by American manufacturers. Why should not American office workers benefit from these technological improvements as well?

## Employers

Employers must become aware of the large body of research documenting office health hazards and implement preventive measures to reduce and eliminate them.

## Government

Congress and the regulatory agencies—federal, state, and local—must ensure effective enforcement of existing health standards in the office. Testing and labelling of hazardous substances must be required by law and enforced. Health standards must be developed for the manufacture and use of video-display terminals. And research agendas, new technologies and standards must be developed to address long-term exposure to low levels of toxic chemicals, high levels of stress, office noise, and the problems of repetitive motion.

### Employees

Finally, employees themselves must take the initiative to become aware of office health hazards, to share their concerns, and to organize for solutions both in the workplace and in the development of public policy.

The full toll of office health hazards is not yet known. But we do know that an epidemic of job-related diseases is certain unless we take steps to reverse it. We must begin to take those steps today.

# 17

## 9 TO 5 AND OTHER SECRETARY LAMENTS AND WORK DAY SONGS

### TALKING 'BOUT MY GENERATION

Just as my generation of secretaries was influenced by television, and the generation before that influenced by the movies — the current generation of secretaries is influenced by contemporary music. In some offices it's easy to spot the secretaries — you just look for the girls in the rock and roll T-shirts. And it's no longer unusual to see someone typing while earphoned to a portable cassette player on the desk.

## OVERWORKED AND UNDERPAID

Given the tremendous popularity of music today, I've decided to put together my SECRETARY'S JUKEBOX, which is a list of songs that are about the wonderful world of work (...or at least songs whose titles have some relevance to the experiences of working people). Oddly enough, there has never been a hit song specifically about what it's like to be a secretary. The closest that we've come to having a secretary's anthem is the following:

## 9 to 5

(Words and music by Dolly Parton)

Tumble out of bed and stumble to the kitchen
Pour myself a cup of ambition
And yawn, and stretch, and try to come to life.
Jump in the shower and the blood starts pumping
Out on the street, the traffic starts jumping
With folks like me on the job from nine to five.

Working nine to five,
What a way to make a living.
Barely getting by, it's all taking and no giving.
They just use your mind and they never give you credit
It's enough to drive you crazy if you let it.

They let you dream just to watch them shatter
You're just a step on the boss man's ladder
But you've got dreams he'll never take away.
In the same boat with a lot of your friends
Waitin' for the day your ship'll come in
And the tide's gonna turn, and it's all gonna roll your way.

Nine to five for service and devotion
You would think that I would deserve a fair promotion.
Want to move ahead but the boss won't seem to let me
I swear sometimes, that man is out to get me.

Nine to five, they've got you where they want you
There's a better life, and you dream about it don't you?
It's a rich man's game, no matter what they call it,
And you spend your life putting money in his pocket.

Courtesy of Velvet Apple Music.
Words and music by Dolly Parton.
©Velvet Apple Music/Fox Fanfare Music Inc. 1980

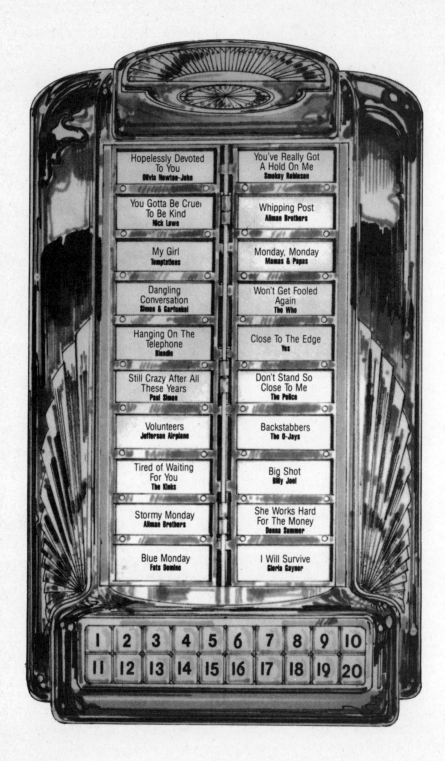

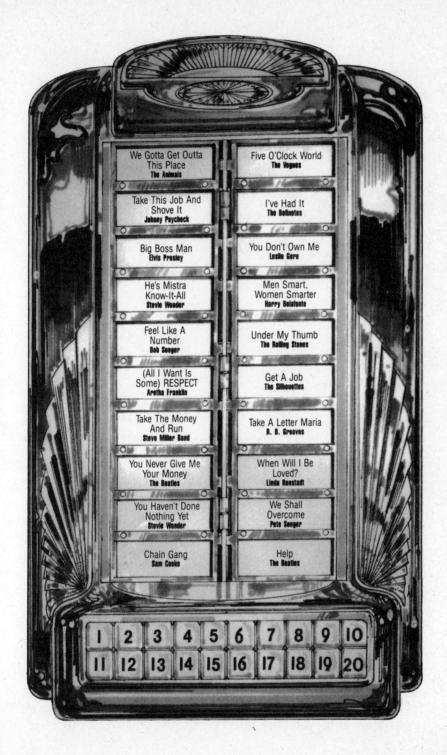

CHAPTER

# 18 OFFICE POLITICS: A SURVIVAL MANUAL FOR SECRETARIES

## THE GAMES PEOPLE PLAY

The first thing that you have to realize about getting ahead in any corporation is that *you have to learn to play the game.* If you're the kind of person who feels that office politics are a demeaning waste of human energy, you're not alone. If you're the kind of person who feels that office politics are a demeaning waste of human energy, and you won't play, you will be alone.

Anyone can make a decision not to get caught up in office politics just as anyone can make a decision not to stay past 5:00 each night. The problem is that either decision will probably relegate you to a life of career mediocrity. That's not to say that some people won't be successful and bypass all the baloney. But most won't. Like it or not, office politics are an inevitable part of your 9 to 5 existence, and you might as well learn to deal with it.

## DEALING WITH YOUR BOSS

As previously discussed, your boss can be either your greatest asset or the greatest impediment to your success. Single-handedly, your boss can give you more status, responsibility, mobility and protection. However, your boss can also get you fired or fix it so that no one in the company even knows you exist. Accordingly, it's important to build a good relationship right from the outset. Here are a few tips that will help you to maximize that relationship:

 Suggest that you and your boss meet periodically to discuss your progress.

 Make sure you understand what your boss' career objectives are and that your boss understands what your career objectives are.

 Let your boss know right from the outset what you are and aren't willing to do.

 It's possible to respect your boss without liking her/him, but it's unlikely that she/he will be as open-minded about you.

# VERWORKED AND UNDERPAID

 Don't extend a social invitation to your boss unless she/he has extended one to you first.

 If there's a party for staff people who assisted on a particular project that you worked on — tell your boss that you'd like to be invited.

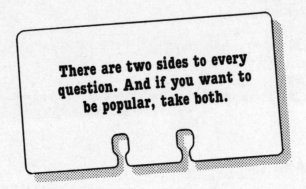

✉ There's a right time to bring things up and a wrong time to bring things up. The person who becomes an expert at distinguishing one from the other will probably succeed in business.

✉ Be loyal to your boss and hope that your boss has the decency to be loyal to you (but don't count on it!).

✉ Don't just go in to your boss to complain. Have a solution already prepared for whatever it is you see as a problem.

> There are two sides to every question. And if you want to be popular, take both.

## DEALING WITH YOUR CO-WORKERS

✉ Newcomers are expected to know their place. Don't be too pushy or too friendly too soon.

✉ Always assume that if you are successful, there will be some people who will be jealous of your success.

✉ Even though it's probably impossible, you should try to get along with everybody. Most offices have a caste system with executives forming one caste and non-executives forming the other. Companies foster these distinctions by creating segregated facilities such as executive dining rooms or executive restrooms. Only one sanctioned activity cuts through all of this and makes everybody equal — the company softball team. If you want to meet people from different departments of the company in a social setting that's a great deal of fun — show up for the softball games. It's a great place to watch your boss screw up and not be able to blame you. And you won't need a program to tell who's who — the executives are the ones with the milk white skin, the dark black socks and the designer sneakers.

✉ Don't expect to make close friends. Like you, everybody else is there to make money and get ahead. If you meet people with whom you develop an enduring friendship, that's great but, don't be surprised if you don't.

## OFFICE ROULETTE

The rules for office roulette are simple. It starts with you screwing something up. Let's say that you were supposed to have made luncheon reservations at Le Hoity Toity for your boss and a party of five important biggies. You forgot, and by the time you realized it, you couldn't beg, borrow or bribe a reservation. It is now the morning of the luncheon and you are ready to confess. But you don't — not if you're a good office roulette player.

A good office roulette player always plays the odds. In this case, chances are 40 to 1 that at least one of the six principals will be forced to cancel the lunch and ask that it be rescheduled to another date.

The truly accomplished roulette player always develops a back-up plan. If you are friendly with one of the five guests invited to the lunch, explain your dilemma and ask them to bail you out by requesting that the lunch be changed to a restaurant closer to their office. If you can't swing that, just book a back-up restaurant.

If it turns out that you have to confess to your mistake, you're no worse off than if you had done it earlier. And, chances are that you'll get away with it without your boss being any the wiser.

✉ Get your name on memos, committee reports and any other documents whenever possible (but only if you've earned the right to have your name mentioned).

✉ Be a good team player.

✉ Involve your co-workers in projects and decision making. Don't be afraid to share the credit.

✉ Don't be afraid to confront people you believe are attempting to short-circuit your career.

✉ Be very careful when you go around somebody or go over somebody's head. It's things like this that truly threaten corporate people, so be sure that you've completely thought through your entire game plan, including possible reprisals from the person scorned.

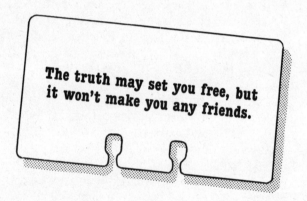

The truth may set you free, but it won't make you any friends.

✉ Find something good to say about other people's ideas but don't be reluctant to offer some constructive criticism when you feel it's appropriate.

✉ Avoid cliques. It's important to have friends that you can rely on, but try not to be branded as a member of any one particular group.

✉ Do favors and use favors: it's the basic rate of exchange in business.

# WHAT OFFICE WORKERS ARE PAID
## IN MAJOR U.S. CITIES

| CITY | FILE CLERK | ACC'T. CLERK | TYPIST/ CLERK | STENO/ TRANSCR. | SEC'Y AVERG. | EXEC. SEC'Y | KEY PUNCH | VDT OPERATOR |
|---|---|---|---|---|---|---|---|---|
| **EASTERN** | | | | | | | | |
| Boston* | $ 7,696 | $10,504 | $ 7,904 | $ 8,528 | $11,596 | $14,144 | $ 9,100 | $ 8,840 |
| Hartford | 7,436 | 9,516 | 8,424 | 8,892 | 10,140 | 13,260 | 8,840 | 9,984 |
| Metro N.J. | 6,864 | 9,724 | 7,904 | 9,828 | 10,556 | 13,520 | 9,256 | 8,528 |
| New York, NY* | 7,072 | 10,712 | 8,372 | 9,516 | 11,544 | 14,716 | 9,672 | 10,296 |
| Pittsburgh | 7,488 | 13,572 | 9,100 | 9,204 | 10,868 | 14,352 | 10,608 | 8,892 |
| Washington, D.C. | 7,800 | 9,724 | 8,164 | 10,764 | 11,128 | 13,780 | 9,464 | 9,828 |
| **EAST CENTRAL** | | | | | | | | |
| Cleveland | 8,372 | 12,740 | 9,048 | 11,024 | 11,596 | 14,144 | 10,296 | 11,076 |
| Detroit Area | 7,072 | 10,764 | 8,736 | 10,348 | 12,948 | 15,340 | 10,088 | — |
| Chicago | 8,009 | 10,688 | 9,007 | 10,738 | 12,273 | 14,878 | 10,354 | — |
| **WEST CENTRAL** | | | | | | | | |
| Minneapolis-St. Paul | 7,124 | 9,672 | 7,696 | 8,684 | 10,140 | 12,636 | 8,892 | 8,580 |
| St. Louis | 7,592 | 9,568 | 7,852 | 8,164 | 9,672 | 11,284 | 8,632 | 8,424 |
| **SOUTHERN** | | | | | | | | |
| Atlanta* | 6,708 | 9,256 | 8,268 | 9,412 | 10,504 | 12,948 | 8,892 | 8,164 |
| Birmingham | 6,708 | 8,632 | 7,436 | 8,996 | 8,684 | 11,232 | 8,320 | 7,332 |
| Louisville | 7,702 | 10,008 | 7,956 | 8,476 | 9,620 | 12,324 | 8,372 | 8,840 |
| Baltimore* | 7,072 | 10,504 | 7,904 | 8,268 | 10,244 | 12,532 | 9,152 | 7,644 |
| Memphis | 6,760 | 9,360 | 7,332 | 7,956 | 9,360 | 12,012 | 8,892 | 8,008 |
| Jacksonville | 6,500 | 8,580 | 6,864 | 7,904 | 9,516 | 11,648 | 8,736 | — |
| Dallas | 6,968 | 10,348 | 8,476 | 10,504 | 11,440 | 13,104 | 9,412 | 9,880 |
| **WESTERN** | | | | | | | | |
| Denver | 7,228 | 12,636 | 9,776 | 12,168 | 12,584 | 15,392 | 10,816 | 9,152 |
| Phoenix | 7,592 | 11,284 | 8,216 | 9,724 | 10,504 | 13,624 | 10,452 | 10,400 |
| San Francisco | 7,176 | 11,544 | 8,892 | 10,452 | 11,960 | 14,924 | 10,400 | 11,804 |
| Seattle | 7,436 | 11,440 | 10,348 | 11,336 | 11,752 | 14,352 | 9,776 | 9,360 |

Source: Office Salaries Directory For the U.S. and Canada, 1979-80, Administrative Management Society as reprinted in a newsletter of 9 to 5 National Association of Working Women.

*The Bureau of Labor Statistics reports generally higher average salaries for these cities when averages from 1978 are adjusted using average increases for 1979 over 1980 cited by the AMS by occupation. See U.S.D.L., B.L.S. Occupational Earnings and Wage Trends in Metropolitan Areas, 1978, S 79-I.

Treat secretaries the way you yourself would like to be treated. When you get somebody's secretary on the phone, say, "Well, I was calling to speak to Ms. Schtummy about the new guidelines on travel reimbursements, but let me ask you because you probably know as much about it as she does."

Beware of people who might try to steal your ideas and take credit for them or people who try to lay off their workload on you.

## HOW SECRETARIES RATE THEIR JOB SATISFACTION

| ASPECT OF JOB | LEVEL OF SATISFACTION | | | |
| --- | --- | --- | --- | --- |
| | Very Satisfied | Somewhat Satisfied | Somewhat Dissatisfied | Very Dissatisfied |
| Overall Satisfaction | 53% | 34% | 10% | 3% |
| Nature and Variety of Work Itself | 54 | 38 | 6 | 2 |
| Level of Responsibility | 35 | 45 | 14 | 6 |
| Opportunity for Advancement | 18 | 33 | 27 | 22 |
| Working Conditions | 55 | 32 | 11 | 2 |
| Salary and Benefits | 33 | 42 | 19 | 6 |

Reprinted by permission, Copyright 1983 The Secretary, official publication of Professional Secretaries International, Kansas City, Mo.

## SOME GENERAL HINTS

Think twice about taking a position that will require you to succeed someone who was extremely well-liked or someone who did a fantastic job; it will be twice as hard for you to distinguish yourself.

It's always helpful to know someone in the personnel department. It's one good way to be able to monitor what's happening at a large company.

Don't be defensive about having gotten your job through nepotism, but don't be cocky about it either.

Act career-minded. If you don't take yourself seriously, no one else will either.

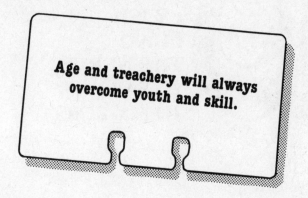 Add short personal notes when you mail out requested materials. Include a sentence or two that demonstrates you understand what the reports are all about.

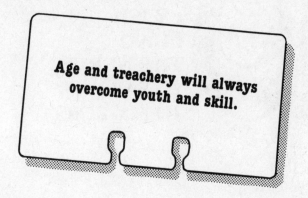 Never, never do anything that is unethical. As this book proves, there are lots of ways to get ahead without stooping to do something you will always regret.

Age and treachery will always overcome youth and skill.

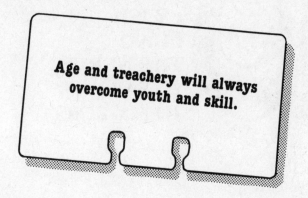 Keep a list of your accomplishments. It will be invaluable to you when you seek to justify a raise or need to write a new résumé.

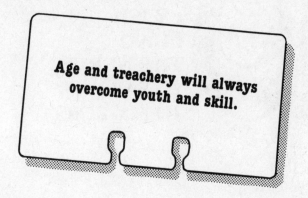 Make sure you have exhausted every possible alternative remedy before filing a grievance with an administrative agency or before initiating a lawsuit.

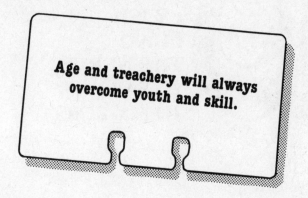 Never assume you can't be fired.

CHAPTER

# 19 SNAPPY THINGS I WISH I HAD THE NERVE TO SAY TO MY BOSS

### ONLY SECRETARIES MAKE MISTAKES

How many times have you heard your boss admit to a mistake? You'll probably hit the state lottery jackpot before that happens! And how many times have you been rebuked or humiliated for something that you didn't do? The next time that happens consider using one of the retorts on the following pages.

## OVERWORKED AND UNDERPAID

# SNAPPY THINGS I WISH I HAD THE NERVE TO SAY TO MY BOSS

# SNAPPY THINGS I WISH I HAD THE NERVE TO SAY TO MY BOSS

# SNAPPY THINGS I WISH I HAD THE NERVE TO SAY TO MY BOSS

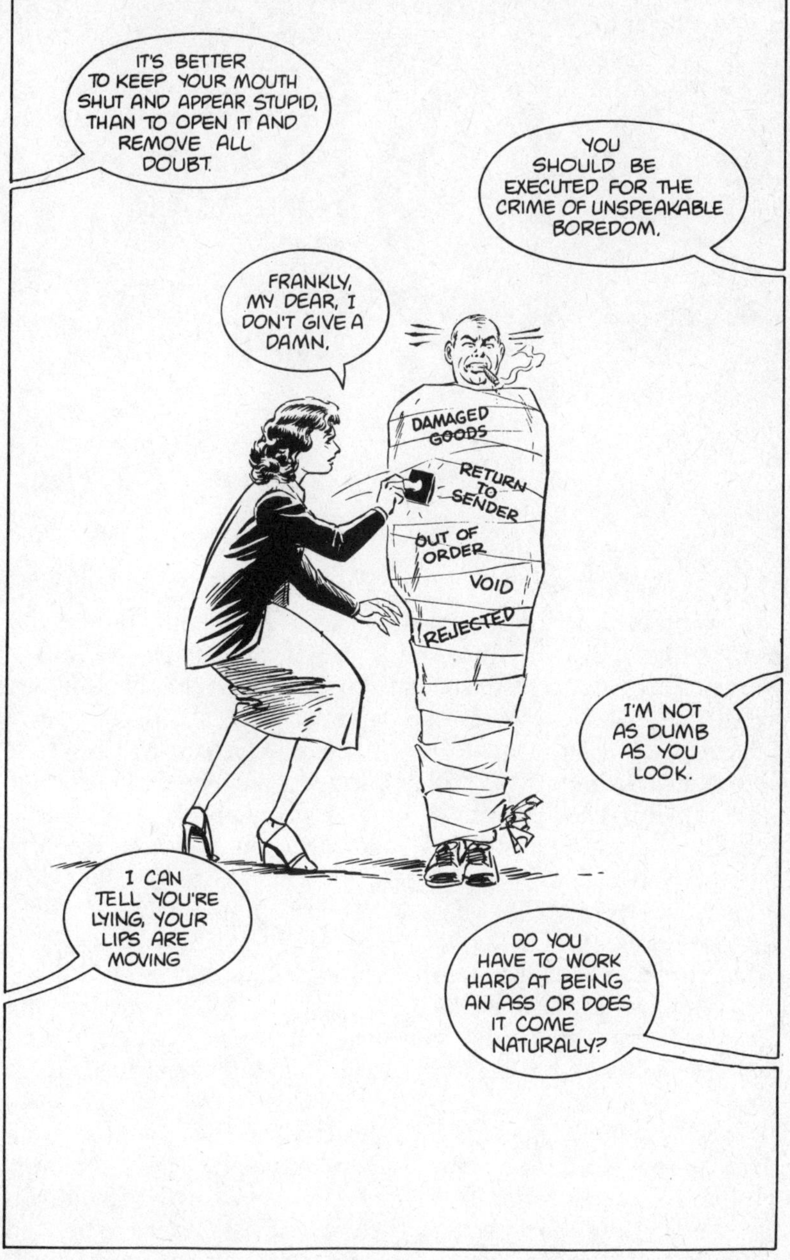

CHAPTER

# 20 HITCHING YOUR WAGON TO A STAR: THE EASY RIDE TO THE TOP

## TICKET TO RIDE

A woman I know has worked with the same company for the past twenty years. Because she is bright, articulate, and has a good performance record, she naturally assumed that her abilities would be rewarded. And, they have been, to a certain extent. Recently, however, a new Chief Executive Officer was brought in to run the company. As often happens, the new CEO brought with him his own Administrative Assistant. The A.A. was a young woman, twenty-one years old, who had only been working for four years. This woman's starting salary was $32,000. My friend's salary (after 20 years with the company) was $26,000. Unfair? I don't think so.

Wittingly or unwittingly, the younger woman has hitched her wagon to a shooting star. Although she had only worked for the CEO for four years, they were the four most successful and meteoric years of that person's career. And her career rose just as far and just as fast.

This so-called "fate-sharing" doesn't always work out so well. And I know more than a few women who have wasted the most productive years of their lives — vicariously living out their own fantasies through their boss. Other women I know have hitched themselves to some real dudskis whose careers are going nowhere.

If you choose to align yourself with someone, make sure they are heading in the right direction.

## THINGS TO LOOK FOR IN AN EXECUTIVE ON THE RISE

(a) Someone who has a corner office.
(b) Someone who is assigned to write important reports.
(c) Someone who is asked to chair certain meetings.
(d) Someone who is repeatedly quoted.
(e) Someone who spends a lot of time in the offices of the top executives and is regularly consulted by them.
(f) Someone who socializes with the decision makers.
(g) Someone who is related to the decision makers.
(h) Someone who is schtupping the decision makers.

# VERWORKED AND UNDERPAID

It's a simple economic fact of life that the highest-paid secretaries generally work for the top-salaried executives. Consequently, riding someone's coattails is at least one valid way to improve your earning potential. But it's not without its down-side risks. Here are some of the pros and cons:

**PRO**: You can escape a lot of the headaches, heartaches and hard knocks of trying to get ahead.

**CON**: By depending upon someone else, you will fail to develop the single most important character trait for success—self reliance.

**PRO**: You will have daily contact with the decision makers of the company — people who can help you further your own career.

**CON**: You may always be overshadowed by your boss and never really appreciated for your own abilities.

**PRO**: You could be vaulted into a world of limousines, private jets and celebrity parties.

**CON**: If you pick the wrong star to hitch your wagon to, you could be sucking down Egg McMuffins for a long time to come.

**PRO**: Working for someone who shifts jobs and/or companies frequently relieves the boredom that inevitably sets in after a few years at the same job.

**CON**: By jumping from company to company you can lose out on credits toward your pension and profit-sharing plans (unless you make it part of your deal when you transfer to the new company).

**PRO**: You may be lucky enough to work for a boss who will assist your career by giving you a great deal of credit and responsibility.

**CON**: You may be unlucky enough to work for someone who takes credit for all of your hard work or someone who intentionally keeps you from advancing so that she/he can retain you as a prized assistant.

**PRO**: After working for the same person for several years, you will have won the trust and support of the boss' husband/wife, who will oftentimes prove to be a valuable ally.

**CON**: After working for the same person for several years, you will inevitably be linked romantically to that person in office gossip, regardless of whether or not it's true.

**PRO**: By working for the same person for several years, each of you will come to appreciate each other's strengths and weaknesses.

**CON**: By working for the same person for several years, each of you will come to appreciate each other's strengths and weaknesses.

# CHAPTER

# 21

## THE SECRETARY'S HALL OF FAME (...FOR THE GREAT AND NEAR GREAT)

MISS BUXLEY · TILLIE · TERRY · BRIDGET · WINNIE · LOLLY

SECRETARY'S HALL of FAME

## THE ENVELOPE, PLEASE

Over the years various women have brought great distinction or notoriety to the role of secretary. I feel that the time has come to honor these individuals in **The Secretary's Hall of Fame**. Here is the list of the honored inductees.

# TELEVISION

**Anne B. Davis -** As Charmain Schultz (Schultzy), secretary to "Love That Bob" (Cummings), Anne B. Davis gave secretaries a role model to admire. Schultzy was bright, warm, funny and very independent (1954).

**Ann Sothern** - As Suzie McNamara in the television show "Private Secretary," Ann Sothern set the style for the stereotype of the fast-thinking, fast-talking secretary who could outwit her bumbling boss any day of the week (1954).

**Barbara Hale** - Perry Mason knew that with his faithful secretary Della Street to back him up, he never had to fear about losing a case to his archrival, prosecutor Hamilton Burger (1957).

# TELEVISION

**Lucille Ball** - After years of playing a nit-wit housewife, Lucille Ball decided to become a nit-wit secretary. As Lucille Carter on the "Here's Lucy" show she worked for her brother-in-law, Mr. Carter (played by Gale Gordon) who owned the Unique Employment Agency. In this photograph Lucy is leading a strike by the secretaries in the office against Mr. Carter (1968).

**Carol Burnett** - A gifted comedienne, Carol Burnett played working class women with great humor and pathos on her "Carol Burnett Show." One of them was a secretary called Mrs. Wiggins. In this photograph Mrs. Wiggins is seen polishing one of her secretarial skills (1967).

**Gail Fisher** - It took until 1968 and a detective show called "Mannix" before the media was willing to acknowledge that some secretaries were black women. Fortunately, the woman who was chosen (Gail Fisher) as well as the character portrayed (Peggy) were strong role models. She is seen here with co-star Mike Connors (1968).

**Marcia Wallace** - Cut from the mold of the acerbic-tongued secretary of early television, Marcia Wallace's character, Carol, did us all proud. Playing the wise-cracking receptionist/secretary, Ms. Wallace constantly upstaged not one, but two male bosses on the very popular "Bob Newhart Show" (1972).

# TELEVISION

**Loni Anderson** — Loni Anderson played the role of Jennifer Marlowe on "WKRP in Cincinnati." As the secretary to the station manager, Loni wasn't exactly your archetypal dumb blonde, but her character would never be confused with a Nobel Laureate either (1978).

**Rita Moreno, Leah Ayres, and Rachel Dennison** - were the sassy and funny secretaries on the television version of "9 to 5." My favorite: Leah Ayres.

# FILM

Dear White Collar Girls:
Here's the first real honest-to-Pitman
picture of you—you fighting for love
and a living in a man's world—you in
your slip and your hair in curlers, all
alone by a telephone that never seems to
ring. It's as candid as the Boss when he
bawls you out—as true-to-life as the talk
in the Ladies' Lounge. It's the big romance you've either had or dreamed about
—from the big best-seller of the year.
                                    —Kitty Foyle

### GINGER ROGERS
*In the First Great Romance of the White Collar Girl*
## 'KITTY FOYLE"
*Christopher Morley's Natural History of a Woman*
*With*
### DENNIS MORGAN • JAMES CRAIG
Eduardo Ciannelli • Ernest Cossart • Gladys Cooper
Directed by **SAM WOOD**
*Who Made "Goodbye, Mr. Chips"*
RKO RADIO PICTURE

Produced by David Hempstead • Harry E. Edington, Executive Producer • Screen Play by Dalton Trumbo and Donald Ogden Stewart

**Ginger Rogers** - Probably the most famous movie ever made about women office workers was, "Kitty Foyle." Although the film was often as overly melodramatic as this movie poster, it won Ginger Rogers the academy award for best actress (1940).

# FILM

**Dorothy McGuire** - One of my favorite movies as a young girl was, "Three Coins In The Fountain." In it audiences got an early glimpse of the liberated woman. The plot involves three women who go to Rome looking for fun and romance. One of the principals, Dorothy McGuire, plays the secretary to an expatriate writer (played by Clifton Webb and pictured here)(1954).

**Janet Leigh**-In the movie, "Psycho," Janet Leigh showed us a darker side of secretaries. Leigh's character, Marion Crane, not only carried on an adulterous affair, but she even embezzled money from her office. In the end, however, Marion discovers that crime doesn't pay as she meets her rather ignominious end in what has become the single most remembered scene in cinema history-the infamous shower scene (1960).

**Karen Lynne Gorney** - One of the largest grossing pictures of all time, "Saturday Night Fever" presented an interesting role model for secretaries in the character of Stephanie (Karen Lynne Gorney). Instead of being thunderstruck by dance partner Tony Manero (John Travolta), Stephanie's primary interest was in using her position as a secretary in a public relations office to advance herself socially and professionally (1977).

**Jane Fonda, Dolly Parton and Lily Tomlin** - Another of the biggest box-office movies ever paid homage to the plight of the secretary. In "9 to 5" these three wonderful women got to live out every secretary's fantasy. . .and then some (1980).

# COMICS

**Winnie Winkle** - The first of the so-called "girl strips," Winnie Winkle was aimed at the growing number of American working women. The strip was started by Martin Branner in 1920 under the title, "Winnie Winkle The Bread-Winner." As a secretary, Winnie was a real inspiration - she was bright, independent and attractive to men. Although Winnie's no longer a secretary and the strip has become something of a soap opera - it's still popular enough to appear in newspapers today (1920).

**Tillie The Toiler** - Tillie was created by Russ Westover in 1921 and ran for thirty-eight years. As the secretary/assistant in a fashion salon, Tillie was the classic working girl (1921).

194

**Lolly -** For better and for worse, Lolly is the kind of character that most people think of when they describe a typical secretary. Along with co-workers Melba and Liz, Lolly experiences the kinds of office crises that many working women can relate to. The strip was created by Pete Hansen (1955).

**Miss Buxley -** Miss Buxley has the distinction of probably being the only comic strip character ever considered *persona non grata* by the women's movement. It's not hard to understand why. As secretary to the General of Camp Swampy in the popular strip "Beetle Baily," Miss Buxley was the consummate "air head." Well endowed (except in the area of brains and skirts), Miss Buxley was the reason that several newspapers decided to drop the Mort Walker-created strip in the late 1970s (1972).

# REAL WORLD

**Rose Mary Woods -** Former President Richard Nixon was probably saved from impeachment by an 18 1/2 minute gap on a tape of a crucial Oval Office discussion on Watergate just two days after the scandal-triggering burglary. One of the only persons to handle that tape was Nixon's personal secretary Rose Mary Woods, shown here at her White House desk (1973).

**Elizabeth Ray -** Probably Washington's most famous secretary, Elizabeth Ray burst onto the scene in 1976. Although she couldn't type, Ms. Ray perfected a horizontal shorthand technique that pleased her boss, Congressman Wayne Hays of Ohio, and several other Washingtonians during her tenure on the Capitol Hill payroll (1976).

**Bridget Carroll** - One of the nice things about being an author is that you can write good things about yourself. Normally I'm a bit more modest but I thought the "Real World" section ought to have at least one secretary who is remembered for the things she did right (1983).

CHAPTER

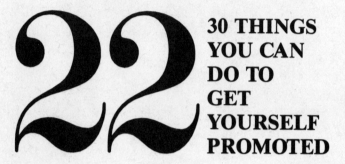

**22**

## 30 THINGS YOU CAN DO TO GET YOURSELF PROMOTED

### SECRETARY OBLIVION

If you've ever seen a chart of a company's executive hierarchy you may have noticed that there are no lines marked "Secretary." This is because a secretarial position is not considered to have any power or mobility. Most secretaries exist in an occupational ghetto from which there is little chance of escape. That's the unfortunate reality of the moment.

### THE MAILROOM OF THE 80s

One of the reasons that I wrote this book (. . .besides making a lot of money!) is to encourage people to use their position as secretaries in such a way as to catapult themselves into better jobs. For years we've had to listen to men drone on about how "I worked my way up to this job by starting in the mail room." I would like the eighties to become the generation that women start to get even with stories of how "I worked my way up to this job by starting as a secretary."

### CAN'T GET THERE FROM HERE

Making the change from secretary to even the most junior executive slot won't be easy. Even though you may already perform all of the functions of someone holding a superior title to your job — it's a quantum leap from here to there. You face the difficult task of not only convincing your bosses that you can do the job but you've got the equally difficult job of convincing yourself.

## ANYTHING HE CAN DO SHE CAN DO BETTER

Many executives try to create a mystique about what it is that they do. Don't let anyone sell you the emperor's new clothes — most jobs are not that difficult to learn (with the exception of a few very technically-oriented occupations). The crucial factor is that you've got to want it badly enough to make some sacrifices and suffer some disappointments.

## GOOD PROSPECTS

The eighties should be a great decade for women in this country. New laws and court decisions all favor the rights of women to equal treatment within the corporate structure. Many companies are making a concerted effort to recruit women, particularly for lower-level management positions. Some companies are doing it because they believe that women employees are every bit as capable as male employees. Others are doing it for public relations reasons or to fulfill some affirmative action quotas. Either way women win.

## ERWORKED AND UNDERPAID

## ASSISTANT TO THE ASSISTANT IN CHARGE OF AS-SISTANTS

If you are a secretary with even the slightest amount of experience you should begin now to position yourself for your next career move. It may be that you want to start by going from the secretarial pool to being an executive secretary. It may be that you already have the knowledge and self-confidence to make the jump to a junior management position. Whatever your goal is—you need a plan (in fact several different plans).


## 30 THINGS TO DO TO GET A PROMOTION OR A RAISE

(. . .or what to do when your career path becomes a narrow trail)

**(1) Be a great secretary.** But don't be so great that your boss begins to believe that she/he can't live without you — if that happens you'll never get promoted.

**(2) Don't hesitate to let your boss know that you are being solicited for another job** (unless, of course, you actually intend to take that job). Nothing I know of makes a boss appreciate an assistant more than the prospect that someone else is about to lure that assistant away with a better job offer.

**(3)Seize the initiative.** One thing that most bosses appreciate is having employees who do things without being told to do them.

**(4) Read what you type.** It's a good way to learn the business and stay informed about what's happening in the office. It may also give you a chance to provide your boss with some of your own ideas on the subject.

**(5) Draft summaries of reports and memoranda.** If you are ambitious (and can spare the time), your boss will really appreciate receiving short summaries of the documents that have been piling up on the desk.

**(6) Confront your boss with the fact that you feel you deserve a promotion.** Be sure to prepare your case ahead of time so that you will have the list of your accomplishments right on the tip of your tongue.

**(7) If you can't get a promotion—get a new title.** As Assistant Production Manager (or whatever) you may not make any more money or do anything differently than you do now—but it can make a big difference, especially if you decide to switch to another company.

**(8) Read the trades or any other important magazine, newspaper or sources of information for your industry.** You'll be surprised at how differently people will react to you when they find that you can speak knowledgeably about their business.

**(9) When your boss gives you a memo for one of his/her superiors, take it to that person yourself** (it's one of the few ways that you can become known by the top bananas).

# WHAT ARE OFFICE WORKERS PAID?

| JOB TITLE | SALARY HISTORY | | | |
|---|---|---|---|---|
| | 1980-81 | 1981-82 | 1982-83 | 1983-84 |
| A. Word Processing Operator | — | 213 | 246 | 253 |
| B. Lead Word Processing Operator | — | 258 | 282 | 289 |
| C. Accounting Clerk— Level B | 141 | 208 | 228 | 241 |
| D. Accounting Clerk— Level A | 227 | 245 | 270 | 286 |
| E. General Clerk— Level B | 169 | 189 | 208 | 224 |
| F. General Clerk— Level A | 204 | 219 | 239 | 258 |
| G. File Clerk | 153 | 168 | 182 | 145 |
| H. Mail Clerk | — | — | — | 209 |
| I. Secretary—Level B | 206 | 219 | 246 | 259 |
| J. Secretary—Level A | 233 | 254 | 276 | 290 |
| K. Executive Secretary —Administrative Assistant | 268 | 293 | 323 | 339 |
| L. Legal Secretary | — | 245 | 286 | 301 |
| M Switchboard Operator/ Receptionist | 193 | 198 | 224 | 233 |
| N. Clerk Typist | 175 | 192 | 213 | 223 |
| O. Customer Service Representative | — | 245 | 260 | 307 |
| P. Photocopy Machine Operator | — | 202 | 220 | 239 |

Source: Office Salary Survey 1983-1984, Administrative Management Society.

**(10) Treat the company's money as parsimoniously as you would treat your own.** Anyone who has ever worked for a large company knows that countless amounts of money are frivolously wasted each day. Don't give in to the "Well, the company can afford it" philosophy. Somebody will notice.

**(11) Take advantage of training programs offered by the company to employees interested in moving up the corporate ladder.**

**(12) Don't leave at 5 o'clock every night.** This is the kind of dedication that usually does not go unnoticed by the powers that be. And eat lunch at your desk—nothing says dedication more than this.

**(13) Make your intentions known.** Let certain people know that you are interested in moving up in the organization so that they will think of you as openings occur.

**(14) Volunteer for assignments.** But do so judiciously (nobody liked the teacher's pet in school; and people like them even less in the business world).

**(15) Be the source of new business.** Naturally, this is easier said than done — unless your family has some clout. And if your family has some clout, what are you doing reading this book?

**(16) Maintain a file of favorable comments.** If you receive thank you notes or favorable comments at the top of letters or reports that you've worked on—be sure to save them. They can prove extremely helpful to you when you are seeking a raise or promotion.

**(17) Be innovative.** I know a woman who made a deal with a travel agency in which she does all of the actual booking of flights, then turns it over to the agency for ticketing. Pursuant to this arrangement, the agency turns back half of its commission to the company. This simple idea alone has saved that company tens of thousands of dollars and won the woman who thought of it a nice promotion and a sizeable bonus.

## THE TONTO DOCTRINE

In the Legend of the Lone Ranger, Tonto became eternally indebted to the masked man because kemo sabe saved his life. Some people think that the same thing can occur in an office situation. It usually happens like this: The boss commits a major screw-up that could jeopardize her/his job or, at the very least, a promotion. The boss has considered all of the executive options (lying, shifting the blame, complete disavowal of the situation) but nothing works under the circumstances.

Then, just when things seem most grim (...
"Tah-dah, Tah-dah. . ") Sally Secretary rides
to the rescue and claims it was all her fault.
Even though she had nothing whatever to do
with the problem (and probably even warned
her boss about it in the first place), Sally is
willing to lay her body across the barbed wire
so her boss can crawl over it and onto the
executive dining-room. In her boss's eye, Sally
is a heroine. In my eyes, Sally is a jerk.

A typical boss is not going to become indebted
to you for life because you took a fall. In fact
you'll be lucky if your heroism is remembered
by the time the bonuses come around next
Christmas. In the meantime, you've probably
set your own career momentum reeling backwards.

Another part of the Tonto Doctrine is the
notion that a secretary will maintain strict
confidentiality regarding any work that she/he
has done for the boss. The latin root for the
word secretary is *secretum* which means secret
and it is an unwritten rule that a secretary will
keep secret anything which she knows about
the boss' affairs.

I think it's important to point out that such
confidentiality is not protected by law as it is
in a situation between a client and a doctor or
lawyer. If your boss commits a crime and you
help her/him or agree not to tell anyone about
it—you run the risk of being a conspirator to that
crime.

My advice on this point is simple. Don't be a
chump. If your boss asks you to cover up —
don't. If you boss asks you to do something
unethical — don't. Just respectfully head for
the door and say, "Hi ho Silver, awwaaaay!"

**(18) Be well-rounded.** One of the principles of survival in the business world is to know a little something about everything. If you simply read Time or Newsweek from cover to cover each week, you'll probably know more about world and national affairs than your boss does.

**(19) Be impatient.** Not with others—but with yourself. More people languish in secretarial jobs because they are unwilling to take the next step. Don't sit around waiting for "the perfect career move" because it will probably never happen unless you make it happen.

**(20) Seize the moment.** Good timing is an absolutely trenchant part of anybody's formula for success. Instead of basking in the glow of writing a report everyone is enthusiastic about, use this time to seek the promotion that you've secretly coveted for the past year.

**(21) Don't be afraid to apply for good jobs that are posted at your company** (regardless of whether or not you feel that other applicants are more qualified than you are). Even if you don't get the job, people are bound to start taking you seriously.

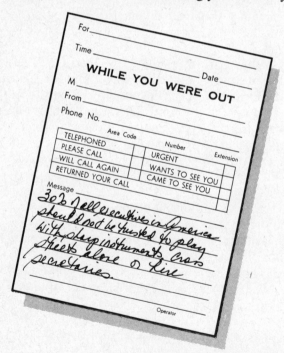

**(22) Take advantage of tuition reimbursement programs.** If the company is willing to pay for training that will help you get ahead, you'd be a fool to turn it down.

**(23) Attend seminars and workshops.** It's a good way to keep abreast of developments in your job field. And it's also a good source of contacts for your next job.

**(24) Make a written record of important meetings.** If your boss promises to give you a raise or promotion (...or even if the boss tells you that she/he will try to get you one)—follow it up with a letter which recounts the terms of what has been agreed to.

**(25) Create a good image.** Remember many bosses choose their assistants more to enhance their own status than based on qualifications or experience.

**(26) Don't use one standard form résumé.** Make up a new one which is tailored specifically for each job you apply for.

**(27) Opt for a job in a money-producing department.** That way if there's a cutback your job will be safer.

**(28) Accept a promotion in title even if it means a drop in salary.** When I took my first non-secretarial job I was forced to accept a cut in salary. It was a sacrifice at the time but once I was on an executive track—I quickly made up the money I lost.

**(29) Be informed.** One way to get people to listen to your ideas is to appeal to their sense of insecurity. Show them that you know what you're talking about. Show them what the competition is doing.

**(30) Remember: Success is achieved by those who seek opportunities—not guarantees.**

## THE JOB CHANGING MYTH

One last thought. Don't be fooled into believing that old shibboleth that, "It looks bad if you change jobs too often." Secretaries like the executives they work for, usually increase their stature and salary by moving from one job to another. Obviously there is a limit to the number of times you can change jobs without running the risk of appearing too flighty or unprofessional. But if each job change shows an increase in responsibility and title, most prospective employers will consider you to have the kind of ambition that they respect.

## THE LAST WORD ON JOBS

Here is a list of jobs that secretarial experience qualifies you for. They are all honest-to-goodness real life job titles taken from the *Dictionary of Occupational Titles* published by the United States Department of Labor.

1. Antisqueak Filler
2. Artificial Inseminator
3. Automatic Brassiere-Slide Making Machine Tender
4. Automatic-Self-Service Station Attendant
5. BB Shot Packer
6. Bird Cage Assembler
7. Bottom Bleacher
8. Bouncer
9. Bowling Ball Finisher
10. Bow Rehairer
11. Caponizer
12. Casket Liner
13. Catheter Builder
14. Character Impersonator
15. Clean-Rice Broker
16. Cremator
17. Creel Clerk
18. Ear-Muff Assembler
19. Goat Herder

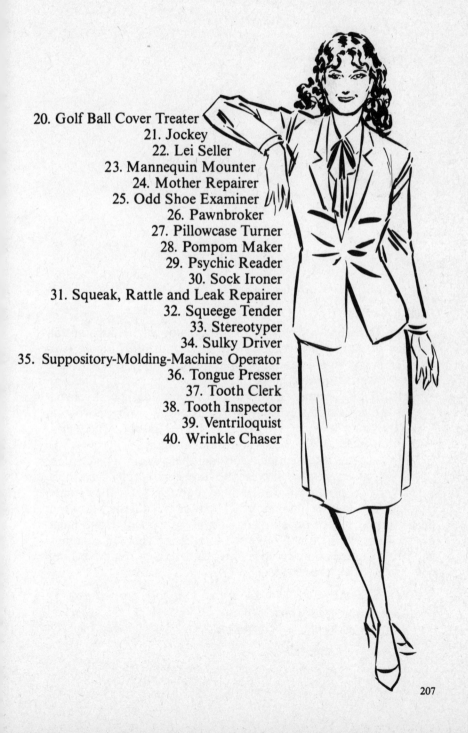

20. Golf Ball Cover Treater
21. Jockey
22. Lei Seller
23. Mannequin Mounter
24. Mother Repairer
25. Odd Shoe Examiner
26. Pawnbroker
27. Pillowcase Turner
28. Pompom Maker
29. Psychic Reader
30. Sock Ironer
31. Squeak, Rattle and Leak Repairer
32. Squeege Tender
33. Stereotyper
34. Sulky Driver
35. Suppository-Molding-Machine Operator
36. Tongue Presser
37. Tooth Clerk
38. Tooth Inspector
39. Ventriloquist
40. Wrinkle Chaser

# CHAPTER

# 23

## A FINAL WORD FOR WOMEN ONLY

## THE EARNINGS GAP

There has been a great deal written about the substantial number of gains that women have made during the past two decades. Magazines, newspapers, and television are filled with stories of women doctors who have achieved important medical break-throughs, women authors who have written best-sellers, women advertising executives who have won awards, women legislators who have been elected to higher public office, and women business owners who have made millions.

The media has also focused a considerable amount of attention upon various women executives who have successfully sued their employers for the right to be paid equally with their male counterparts in those companies. In light of all the attention given to these accomplishments, it's not surprising that most people (women included) have the impression that the earnings gap between men and women is practically non-existent. Nothing could be further from the truth.

*In 1961 women who worked at full-time jobs earned only 59 cents for every dollar earned by men. By 1977, after 16 years of the women's movement, this number had not changed by even one penny!*

# REASONS FOR THE MALE-FEMALE EARNINGS GAP

Among the explanations offered for the vast differential between men and women's salaries are:

(a) The majority of women are still concentrated in lower paying occupations of a traditional nature that provide limited opportunity for advancement (*approximately one-third of all full-time working women make less than $10,000 per year!*)

(b) The recent dynamic rise of women's participation in the labor force has resulted in a large number of women who are in or near entry level positions.

(c) Although women workers are as well educated as men in terms of median years of schooling completed, they often receive education, training and counseling which directs them into traditional and low-paying jobs.

(d) Since working women with family responsibilities tend to work less overtime—this results in lower total earnings for women.

(e) Women tend to have fewer years of work-life experience than men.

Even after adjusting for these and other factors such as age, region and industrial concentration, the U.S. Department of Labor says that "much of the female-male earnings differential remains unexplained." As far as I'm concerned the problem can be explained in a few words — discrimination by men and the passivity of women.

## ERWORKED AND UNDERPAID

## DISCRIMINATION BY MEN

### ENOUGH IS ENOUGH!

The discrimination by men against women in the work place

is so well documented that I doubt any reasonable person would disagree that it has and does exist. The disturbing thing is that this form of financial prejudice is no less pervasive today than it was twenty years ago. The time has come for working women to say, "Enough!" and fight for the equality that they are entitled to under the law.

## THE EQUAL PAY ACT

The Equal Pay Act provides that it's against the law for an employer to pay a woman less than a man for doing substantially the same work if the jobs require equal skill, effort and responsibility. Women who think that they have been the victim of this type of discrimination are usually encouraged to contact the Equal Opportunity Commission.

It sounds easy doesn't it? Contact the Equal Employment Opportunity Commission, just pick up the phone, the people from Washington arrive the next day, your boss acknowledges that he made a terrible mistake, he pays you five thousand dollars in back wages and then thanks you for calling in the federal authorities to straighten him out on this point. Sure it works that way — in one out of every ten billion cases!

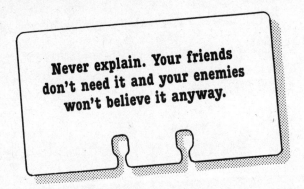

Never explain. Your friends don't need it and your enemies won't believe it anyway.

## EXERCISING YOUR RIGHTS

In Appendix A I've outlined a whole series of protections that are granted to women under the laws of the United States. But having the rights is only half the battle — having the ability to exercise those rights is the other half. If a woman believes that by complaining to a governmental agency she's likely to get fired, that woman is going to keep her mouth shut. If a woman believes that the only way she can enforce her rights is through a costly, time-consuming court litigation, that woman is not going to get involved. Some executive level women maybe choose to stand and fight, but most working class women will not — they will be forced to make their decision based on practical pocket-book constraints.

## BEING PRACTICAL

Being practical is not necessarily a bad strategy and under certain circumstances it's probably the best way to proceed. Let me give you an example of what I mean. Under the law, an employer is not supposed to ask the following questions when considering someone for employment:

Are you married?

How many children do you have? What are their ages?

Are you pregnant?

You could refuse to answer these questions, in which case you would probably not get the job. If you filed a complaint, the employer will probably deny asking you the questions or claim that someone with superior credentials was hired. Either way you lose. Even if you lie in order to get the job, the employer will then simply look for other ways to fire you once she/he learns the truth.

In a situation like this I think it's best to be practical. The fact of the matter is that a woman who is pregnant or a woman with small children is not likely to be able to put in the same amount of work hours as someone with no children. In addition to being unavailable for overtime, the typical working mother will lose a certain number of days because of chicken pox, out of school suspensions and babysitters who fail to show up. As a working mother you need to work for an employer who is flexible and understanding of these types of situations. If the employer is going to give you a hard time about it—I think it's better to find out right away and look for a different job.

# THE PASSIVITY OF WOMEN

## GET UP, STAND UP FOR YOUR RIGHTS

It's important that working women distinguish between being practical and shrinking from their responsibility to stand up for their rights. For example, if an employer was demanding sexual favors in return for raises or promotions — a woman would be doing a great disservice to herself and her fellow workers by failing to report such an incident. Practically speaking nothing may ever come of the charges and the woman might be subjected to tremendous humiliation or worse. But if women in these situations don't start to speak up — nothing will ever change. Employers rely on the fact that most women are too passive *or* too docile to offer anything more than token resistance. So far the employers have been right. . . . . . .so far.

## SAFETY IN NUMBERS

The key to success in these situations is to join forces with other women at your company who are experiencing similar problems. For one thing it makes your case a lot stronger if you have to eventually go to court in order to prove your allegations. And for another, it makes it harder for your boss to fire you (there *is* safety in numbers). But whatever you do, don't do anything until you get some good advice. Consult a lawyer, contact a women's group or any person or organization who can explain your rights, analyze your case, and give you some good advice on how to proceed.

Just when you thought you were winning the rat race, along comes faster rats.

## THE NORMA RAE APPROACH

Exercising your legal rights or taking a practical approach are two ways to deal with discrimination in the workplace. There's one other way. Unionize. Although many women are unaware of it, there are a few different unions interested in organizing secretaries and other clerical workers. Two of the most active are: District 925 of the Service Employees International Union at 2020 K Street, N.W., Washington, D.C. 20006 and the American Federation of State, County and Municipal Employees at 1625 L Street N.W., Washington, D.C. 20036.

According to the District 925's statistics, office workers who belong to unions earn 32% more than those who are not unionized. I have mixed feelings about whether or not a union is the solution (which it can be) or just another part of the problem (which it can also be). The important thing is that you understand that federal and state law strongly protect your right to

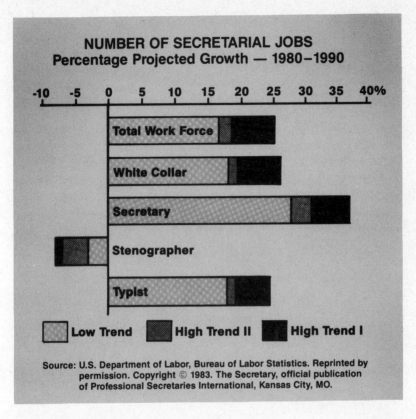

**NUMBER OF SECRETARIAL JOBS**
Percentage Projected Growth — 1980–1990

-10 -5 0 5 10 15 20 25 30 35 40%

Total Work Force

White Collar

Secretary

Stenographer

Typist

☐ Low Trend    ▨ High Trend II    ■ High Trend I

Source: U.S. Department of Labor, Bureau of Labor Statistics. Reprinted by permission. Copyright © 1983. The Secretary, official publication of Professional Secretaries International, Kansas City, MO.

organize, and your employer cannot fire you or discriminate against you for forming a union or otherwise taking group actions to improve your working conditions. I think it's definitely worth looking into.

## WORKING FOR WOMEN

As a woman who has worked on both sides of the desk I am ashamed to acknowledge that a working woman's biggest enemy is often a woman executive. A few years ago some psychologists dubbed this phenomena as "The Queen Bee Syndrome." What they found was that women who advanced into executive positions were less likely than men to treat their secretaries and other female assistants with respect. The psychologists determined that these women executives were protective of their own gains and didn't want to risk losing any of their hard won power to another woman.

Unless women executives are willing to treat the women who work for them with the same sense of fairness they themselves demand from their male colleagues, then the women's movement is destined to fall on its white-collar face. If women can't be respectful toward other women and help each other to succeed, how can they possibly expect men to treat them with respect or to help them?

## WORKING FOR MEN

I don't want to imply that women have cornered the market on treating secretaries like dirt: men have had considerably more practice at it and some have developed it into an art form. The male bosses to avoid are the ones who say things like, "Well, don't worry your pretty little head about it: or "My girl will call your girl about scheduling a time for us to get together."

I think the real solution for dealing with these people is *don't let them get to you.* If someone asks you for the woman's point of

```
For _____ Date _____
Time _____
        WHILE YOU WERE OUT
M _____
From _____
Phone No. _____
        Area Code        Number        Extension
┌─────────────────┬─────────────────────────────┐
│                 │ URGENT                       │
│ TELEPHONED      │ WANTS TO SEE YOU             │
│ PLEASE CALL     │ CAME TO SEE YOU              │
│ WILL CALL AGAIN │                              │
│ RETURNED YOUR CALL                             │
└─────────────────┴─────────────────────────────┘
Message _____
```

The women's movement raised an issue over secretaries serving coffee. Hell, that's the easy part; it's cleaning the damn pot and filthy cups that's the real pain in the butt.

        Operator

view on a subject, say what you think but let it be known that you regard it as a position everyone should subscribe to. If a fellow woman in the office makes a mistake and someone attributes it to the fact that she is a woman "no reflection on you, of course," don't get hysterical. If you react emotionally in situations like this, you will be helping to perpetuate the myth that women don't react well to criticism or that they are not stable as male employees. In a situation like the one described, I would simply point out to the numbskull who made the remark that there have been a number of significant mistakes made by some of the men in the company and that everyone should by evaluated on her or his own merits rather than by grouping people into gender categories.

## GETTING AHEAD AS A WOMAN

The simple philosophy of this book is this: if you want to get ahead, you've got to look, act and think the part. If you dress like a low-paid secretary, you will be paid like a low-paid secretary. If you don't let people know you are capable of doing more than typing and pouring coffee, you will be typing and pouring coffee for a long time.

Until recently, women were always conditioned to believe that they couldn't compete with men — physically, emotionally or intellectually. Fortunately that's beginning to change. Twenty years ago when I took my first job as a receptionist I never even dreamed that I could win a managerial level position. Ten years ago I started dreaming about it. And two years ago I went ahead and did it.

The simple truth that it took me all those years to learn is that women can compete with men — if they are willing to take chances. *I think that most women fail to succeed in their careers*

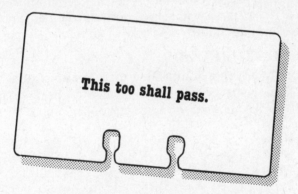

This too shall pass.

*because they are unable or unwilling to take risks.*

In this book I have outlined a number of strategies for how to position yourself in order to get a better job or a promotion. The truth of the matter is that anything I've written here is useless if you are going to be afraid to try it for fear of failing or even for fear of trying something new. In the end, college degrees, self-help books, and professionally written résumés are all worthless if you don't have the confidence in your own abilities and the willingness to take a chance.

## WHAT HAPPENS WHEN YOU START MAKING MORE MONEY THAN YOUR HUSBAND OR YOUR BOY-FRIEND?

Some books spend a lot of time on the psychology of how to deal with the situation of the woman making more money than her husband or boyfriend. My advice is straight-forward: if in the 1980s you've got a husband or boyfriend who feels threatened because you make more money than he does, you've got the wrong husband or boyfriend.

## A FINAL WORD

During the next few years the power of working women will grow at an unprecedented rate. Women who worked their way into upper management during the past decade will finally be in policy making positions. Legal precedents in sex discrimination cases will make it easier for women to exercise their rights and be treated equally. And there will be a whole new generation of women coming in to the workforce who have not been brain-washed into thinking that they are inferior to men.

It will be a particularly good time for women who are secretaries. The U.S. government projects that there will approximately 300,000 new jobs opening up in this area each year. And many of those jobs will involve the processing of information which means that secretaries will be well positioned for advancement as we move from an industrial society to an informational society.

## ......NO—THREE WORDS

There are just three things that a person must do who hopes to go from being a low-paid secretary to being a high-paid secretary to having your own secretary—and those three things are:

   1. WORK
   2. WORK
   3. WORK

COMPLETED

216

# APPENDIX A

## HOW WOMEN CAN ASSERT THEIR JOB RIGHTS

The first step in asserting your legal rights is to know what those rights are. It is important to know which unfair or discriminatory practices are prohibited by law, and to distinguish these from actions which may seem unjust, but which are not unlawful.

You should also keep in mind that an employer can take action against an employee for good cause. Laws that protect against discrimination based on race, color, sex, national origin, religion, age, or handicap do not prevent an employer from discharging you if you are not doing your job; nor do they require employers to hire you if you are not qualified for the job.

You can resolve many problems associated with getting a job or coping with a particular job situation through discussion with personnel officers or supervisors. Informal problem solving is frequently the quickest method for settling a dispute; often the problem arises because of misunderstanding, lack of communication, or ignorance of the employee's rights. In many work establishments, informal conciliation is part of grievance procedures under collective bargaining agreements, personnel policies, or formal equal employment opportunity programs.

However, if you believe that you are being paid less than a legal wage, or are a victim of discrimination prohibited by law, you are entitled to file a complaint with the agency that has responsibility for enforcing the law. Procedures for making complaints vary; a telephone request is enough to set in motion an investigation into substandard wages or unequal pay, whereas a written complaint is necessary under some antidiscrimination laws.

If you feel that you are being treated unfairly, take care to document incidents to support a complaint. Written notes on what happened and when, and who was there, are very useful in refreshing the memory and showing a pattern of unfair treatment.

There are time limits on filing complaints, so it is important to act promptly. Information about time limits and procedures under the various laws is provided with each section in this chapter. If you are unsure about how the law might apply to a specific situation, call the agency that handles those complaints to talk with compliance officers who are trained to provide information about filing complaints.

Addresses of compliance agencies as well as agencies which administer laws on retirement or disability, for example, are listed in Appendix B.

In addition, most agencies with enforcement or administrative responsibilities for Federal laws print pamphlets with information for consumers. Free copies of these materials are generally available from the agency upon request. Additional sources of assistance and information exist in the form of community based organizations that have information and referral, counseling, or legal assistance services. The local bar association, a State or local commission on women, or an information and referral center may be able to provide information about these resources.

## YOUR JOB RIGHTS

Workers are protected on the job by a variety of laws which prohibit discrimination and govern wages, hours, occupational safety and health and other employment-related issues. The following is a list of your most important job rights and what you should do to assert them.

## MINIMUM WAGES AND OVERTIME PAY

The Fair Labor Standards Act (FLSA) provides for minimum wages and overtime pay for covered workers. The FLSA now covers the majority of workers. However, casual babysitters and companions for the aged and infirm, executive, administrative, and professional employees, outside salespeople and agricultural workers are still exempt from both the minimum wage and overtime premium pay provisions of the FLSA. (Extension of these provisions to State and local government workers in areas of traditional governmental functions was declared unconstitutional by the U.S. Supreme Court.)

Since January 1981, the minimum hourly rate for all covered workers has been $3.35 for the first 40 hours each week (workers in some States benefit from higher rates under State laws). Under certain conditions lower rates may be paid to learners, apprentices, handicapped workers, and full-time students.

The FLSA does not limit the hours of work for employees who are 16 years old or older. However, most covered workers are entitled to 1½ times their regular rate of pay for hours in excess of 40 a week. The law does not require premium pay for overtime for covered agricultural workers, live-in household workers, taxicab drivers, and employees of motor carriers, railroads, and airlines. Hospitals, nursing homes, and rest homes may compute overtime after 8 hours a day or after 80 hours in a 14-day period.

The law permits lodging, board, or other facilities provided by an employer to be considered as a part of wages. Also tips actually received and retained may be counted for up to 40 percent of the minimum wage. The tip credit can be claimed only for workers who are engaged in an occupation in which they customarily and regularly receive tips of more than $30 a month.

The Federal law does not require premium pay for weekends or holiday work, or, generally, for daily overtime; nor does it require rest periods, discharge notices, or severance pay. It is enforced by the Wage and Hour Division of the Employment Standards Administration, U.S. Department of Labor, which has authority to investigate complaints and to initiate action against violators of the law who may be subject to civil or criminal court action.

Some States have laws limiting the days per week an employee can be required to work or which contain provisions on Sunday work, working on the Sabbath, holidays, and rest periods. The State department of labor can provide information about its employment laws.

Provisions of a collective bargaining agreement or written personnel policies may provide similar or additional benefits with some employers.

### What To Do

If you think that you are not being paid the minimum wage or required overtime pay, you may file a complaint with the Wage and Hour Division in Washington, D.C., or at one of the regional offices. (See Appendix B for addresses.) Complaints are treated confidentially.

Upon receiving a complaint of an FLSA violation, Wage and Hour compliance officers investigate to see if it is valid. If it is, the Wage and Hour Division attempts to persuade the employer to comply with the law. If these attempts are unsuccessful, the case is referred to the Department of Labor Solicitor's Office, which may decide to file suit against the employer in Federal court.

In addition to the Federal remedy, under FLSA you have a right to sue the employer yourself for back pay, damages, attorney's fees and court costs. However, if you begin a private suit, the Department of Labor will not pursue your case in court. In order to recover back pay, you must file your suit in court within 2 years, except in cases of willful violations, in which case the time limit is 3 years.

It is unlawful to discharge or otherwise discriminate against an employee for filing a complaint or participating in a proceeding under the FLSA.

## EQUAL PAY

The Equal Pay Act of 1963 amended the FLSA to prohibit unequal pay for women and men who work in the same establishment and whose jobs require equal skill, effort, and responsibility. Pay differences based on a seniority or merit system or on a system that measures earnings by quantity or quality of production are permitted. Employers may not reduce the wage rate of any employee in order to eliminate illegal wage differences. The law is interpreted as applying to "wages" in the sense of all employment-related payments, including overtime, uniforms, travel, and other fringe benefits.

In addition to covering employees subject to the minimum wage requirements of the FLSA, the law applies to Federal, State and local government employees; executive, administrative, and professional employees; and outside salespeople.

A number of court cases have established that jobs need be only substantially equal, not identical, in order to be compared for purposes of the act, job descriptions or classifications are irrelevant in showing that work is unequal, unless they accurately reflect actual job content, and mental as well as physical effort must be considered.

### What To Do

If you think you are not receiving equal pay for equal work, you may file a complaint with the Equal Employment Opportunity Commission, which enforces the Equal Pay Act. Under ordinary circumstances, your identity will not be revealed during an investigation of an alleged equal pay violation. If a violation is found, EEOC will negotiate with the employer for a settlement including back pay and appropriate raises in pay scales to correct the violation of the law. EEOC may also initiate court action to collect back wages under the act.

Under the Equal Pay Act you also have a right to sue privately for back pay, damages, attorney's fees, and court costs. However, you may not sue the employer if you have already been paid full back wages under EEOC supervision or if EEOC has filed a suit in court to collect these wages. You must file suit within 2 years of Equal Pay Act violation, except in the case of willful violations, in which case there is a 3-year time limit.

## PAY EQUITY

In 1981, the U.S. Supreme Court ruled that the prohibition of sex-based wage discrimination in title VII of the Civil Rights Act is not limited to claims of equal pay for equal work. Most women workers are concentrated in relatively few occupations. Some who work in traditionally female jobs have filed complaints under title VII, charging that such work is undervalued and underpaid in comparison with other work — generally performed by men — different in content but seen to require the same or less educational preparation, experience, skill, and responsibility. For example, nurses have questioned their pay compared to that of city sanitarians, and clerical employees have claimed discrimination in comparing their wages to those of physical plant employees. This is a developing area of the law, and it is not yet clear what practices courts will rule amount to sex-based wage discrimination under title VII.

## PROMOTIONS, TRAINING, AND WORKING CONDITIONS

Title VII of the Civil Rights Act of 1964 also protects workers against discrimination on the basis of sex, race, color, religion, or national origin in most on-the-job aspects of employment. Employers must recruit, train, and promote persons in all job classifications without discrimination. Promotion decisions must be made according to valid requirements. Training and apprenticeship opportunities must be offered in accord with equal employment opportunity principles. Employers may not discriminate against individuals on any terms or conditions or privileges of employment.

Similar protections are provided to employees of Federal contractors and subcontractors under Executive Order 11246, as amended. (See section on "Discrimination Based on Sex, Race, Color, Religion, and National Origin. ") Under the affirmative action order for service and supply contractors, employers are required to set goals and timetables for promoting women and minorities.

On-the-job protection for handicapped workers is provided under sections 501, in the case of Federal employment, and 503 and 504 of the Rehabilitation Act of 1973. The Age Discrimination in Employment Act protects workers from on-the-job discrimination based on age.

## What To Do

If you think you have been treated unfairly on the job, and the basis for the action was your sex, race, color, religion, national origin, handicap, or age, you may contact the agency that enforces the law for more information about the protections provided and the enforcement process. You can find out how to file a complaint and what your legal rights are. The laws prohibit employers from discharging or otherwise discriminating against individuals who file complaints or participate in an enforcement process.

## MATERNITY LEAVE/PREGNANCY DISCRIMINATION

Title VII of the Civil Rights Act of 1964 as amended in 1978 specifically prohibits discrimination because of pregnancy. Employers cannot refuse to employ a woman because of pregnancy or terminate her, force her to go on leave at an arbitrary point during pregnancy, or penalize her because of pregnancy in reinstatement rights — including credit for previous service, accrued retirement benefits, and accumulated seniority.

The law does not require and employer to provide a specific number of weeks for maternity leave, or to treat pregnant employees in any manner different from other employees with respect to hiring or promotions, or to establish new medical leave, or other benefit programs where none currently exist.

The law requires that women affected by pregnancy, childbirth or related medical conditions be treated the same for all employment-related purposes, including receipt of benefits under fringe benefit programs, as persons not so affected but similar in their ability or inability to work. The amendment does not require employers to pay for health insurance benefits for abortions, except where the life of the mother would be endangered or where medical complications have arisen from an abortion.

Pregnant workers in a number of States are entitled to benefits under statewide temporary disability insurance laws, special sections of fair employment of labor codes, and regulations or court decisions interpreting statutory bans on sex discrimination in employment. You can check with the department of labor or human or civil rights agencies listed in Appendix B for information about your rights to fringe benefits under State laws.

## What To Do

If you think you are being treated unfairly because your temporary inability to work is due to pregnancy, you should contact the Equal Employment Opportunity Commission office that serves your area for information about your right under title VII. (See Appendix B for addresses.)

## SEXUAL HARASSMENT

Sexual harassment is an unlawful employment practice under title VII of the Civil Rights Act of 1964, as amended. The EEOC "Guidelines on Discrimination Because of Sex" provide that unwelcome sexual advances, requests for sexual favors, and other verbal or physical conduct of a sexual nature constitutes sexual harassment when:

Submission to such conduct is made either explicitly or implicitly a term or condition of an individual's employment.

Submission to or rejection of such conduct by an individual is used as the basis for employment decisions affecting that person.

Such conduct has the purpose or effect of unreasonably interfering with an individual's work performance or creating an intimidating, hostile, or offensive working environment.

Under the Guidelines, an employer, employment agency, joint apprenticeship committee, or labor organization is responsible for the acts of its agents and supervisory employees, regardless of whether the specific acts complained of were forbidden and regardless of whether the employer knew of their occurrence. An employer is also responsible for sexual harassment by co-workers where the employer knew or should have known of the conduct, unless immediate and appropriate corrective action was taken. An employer may also be responsible for sexual harassment by clients or customers.

## What To Do

If you are being sexually harassed, you can contact the Equal Employment Opportunity Commission for information and assistance in filing a sex discrimination complaint under title VII. In sexual harassment cases it is particularly important to keep a record of incidents of harassment.

A victim of sexual harassment can also file a suit under State laws which protect against assault, battery, intentional infliction of emotional distress, or intentional interference with an employment contract.

If the sexual harassment subjects the person being harassed to sexual contact, it could be a violation of criminal law against sexual assault. In addition, women in one case were able to seek redress under the National Labor Relations Act.

For more information, contact the Equal Employment Opportunity Commission (see Appendix B for address) or the Women's Bureau, U.S. Department of Labor, Washington, D.C., 20210, for a list of resources.

## GARNISHMENT

Garnishment is a procedure through which a creditor (such as a department store, finance company or recipient of court-ordered child support or alimony payments) can collect money owed; and the creditor can reach property of the debtor which is held by a third party (such as bank or an employer). The most common form of garnishment is wage garnishment, where a creditor can go to court to get an order to have a portion of the debtor's wages paid directly to the creditor. Debtors are protected in garnishment proceeding by title III of the Consumer Credit Protection Act, which is enforced by the Wage and Hour Division of the U.S. Department of Labor. The law limits the amount of disposable income which may be taken in garnishment proceeding, and protects workers from being fired because of garnishment of any one indebtedness.

Many States have garnishment laws with provisions which offer greater protection than the Federal law does. For information about State laws, contact the State department of labor or consumer protection agency. For information about the Federal law, contact the Wage and Hour Division of the U.S. Department of Labor. (See Appendix B for addresses.)

## UNEMPLOYMENT INSURANCE

Unemployment insurance is a weekly benefit paid for a limited time to eligible workers when they are involuntarily unemployed. The purpose of the payment is to tide unemployed workers over until they find jobs for which they are reasonably suited in terms of training, past experience, and past wages. Benefits are paid in cash as a matter of right, and are not based on need. Unemployment insurance is a Federal-State system under which the Federal law establishes certain minimum requirements, but each State administers its own program. State law determines who is eligible, how much money each person receives, and how long benefits will be paid. To be eligible, a person must be unemployed, able to work, and available for and seeking work.

In most States benefits are paid out of a fund collected from a special tax on employer payrolls. The amount of each employer's tax varies according to the amount of unemployment benefits paid to former employees. The Federal Government provides funds for payments to its laid-off civilian and for persons discharged from the Armed Forces.

Almost all workers are covered by unemployment insurance. While each State specifies the amount of weekly and total payments and the manner in which they are calculated, the usual result is that the jobless worker receives about 50 percent of the average weekly wage formerly received. Most States limit payment to a maximum duration of 26 weeks, although some continue as long as 28 to 39 weeks. A special program provides that during times of high unemployment in the State, individuals who have exhausted their benefits under State law may continue to receive payments for up to 13 additional weeks. Unemployment payments may be taxable if an individual's adjusted gross income reaches a certain level, depending on State and Federal income tax reporting requirements.

Each State has its own rule about who is not qualified to receive benefits. Voluntary quits without good cause and being fired for misconduct are the two major reasons for disqualification. Another is refusal to accept a suitable job without good cause. The individual who is refused benefits is given a report indicating why benefits will not be paid and how long the disqualification will last. Penalties can range from postponement to denial of benefits for the duration of the current period of unemployment. States cannot deny benefits solely on the basis of pregnancy or recency of pregnancy, but pregnant individuals do have to meet the generally applicable requirements of seeking work and being available for and able to work. Persons who leave their jobs because of sexual harassment may be able to show they quit for good cause. Successful actions have been brought in a number of States in which women were held eligible for unemployment benefits after leaving a job because of sexual harassment.

Many States have provisions which disqualify workers who quit for reasons not attributable to the work or the employer. A number of other States disqualify workers for leaving the job for family reasons, such as getting married, moving with a spouse, or child care problems. Some States, however, will pay benefits to persons who quit their jobs for compelling personal reasons, and make decisions about benefit payments on a case-by-case basis according to the individual circumstances.

The requirement that a worker be available for employment

in order to be eligible for unemployment compensation benefits presents problems for part-time workers in most States. This is because "available for employment" is interpreted to mean available for full-time employment. In most cases the requirements for full-time availability is the result of administrative interpretation, rather than provisions in the legislation. In a few States, unemployed persons who can work part time only will be considered "available" (and eligible for unemployment compensation) if they have been working in an occupation in which there is substantial demand for workers.

For information about unemployment benefits and eligibility requirements in your State, contact the employment security office that serves your area. Addresses are included in the telephone directory under State government listings.

## COMPENSATION FOR INJURIES

Workers who are injured on the job or who contract an occupational disease may receive compensation under State workers' compensation laws. These laws provide for prompt payment of benefits to injured workers with a minimum of red tape and without the necessity of fixing the blame for the injury. In most States employers are required by law to cover their employees with workers' compensation protection, and heavy penalties are assessed for failure to comply with the law.

Since each State has its own law and operates its own system, the employees covered, the amount of compensation, duration of benefits, and procedures for making and settling claims vary widely. There are time limits within which notice of injury must be given to the employer, and failure to notify within the specified time will bar a claim. Benefits can include medical payments for the period of disability or for permanent disability, rehabilitation services, death benefits to a worker's family, and burial expenses. Some States have awarded workers' compensation for disability caused by work-related stress, including stress related to alleged sexual discrimination. Compensation payments are generally financed through private insurance companies, State compensation funds, or self-insurance by employers. For more information about workers, compensation benefits and procedures, write to the State department of labor or industrial commission.

Federal workers and certain other workers are coverd by Federal workers' compensation laws. The Office of Workers' Compensation Programs in the U.S. Department of Labor administers the Federal Employees Compensation Act, and Mine Safety and Health

Act, and the Longshoremen's and Harbor Workers Compensation Act. For information about these programs, contact the Office of Workers' Compensation Program, U.S. Department of Labor, Washington, D.C. 20210.

## OCCUPATIONAL SAFETY AND HEALTH

The Occupational Safety and Health Act of 1970 is designed to ensure safe and healthful working conditions throughout the Nation. It covers every employer in a business affecting commerce, except where the workplace is covered under a special Federal law such as those for the mining and atomic energy industries. Federal employees are covered by an Executive order, and State and local government employees may be covered by the State, operating under a plan approved by the Federal Government. The law encourages States to operate occupational safety and health programs by providing grants for those whose plans demonstrate that the program can be "at least as effective as" the Federal program.

Under the general duty clause of the law, each employer must provide a workplace free from recognized hazards that are causing or are likely to cause death or serious physical harm. The Occupational Safety and Health Administration (OSHA) of the U.S. Department of Labor establishes standards which require conditions or the use of practices or methods necessary to protect workers on the job. OSHA has issued standards on the following substances: acrylonitrile, inorganic arsenic, asbestos, benzene, 14 carcinogens, coke oven emissions, cotton dust, Dibromochloropropane (DBCP), lead, and vinyl chloride. It is the employer's responsibility to become familiar and comply with the standards, to put them into effect, and to assure that employees have and use personal protective equipment required for safety and health.

Employees have a right to:
- request that OSHA conduct an inspection if they believe hazardous conditions or violations of standards exist in their workplace
- file a written request for an immediate inspection whenever they fear that an imminent danger is present in the workplace. If OSHA decides an inspection is unnecessary, they must notify the employee in writing
- refuse in good faith to expose themselves to a hazardous condition if there is no reasonable alternative. The condition must be of such a nature that, to a reasonable person, there is a real danger of death or serious injury and there is not enough time to do away

with the danger through the complaint process
- have an authorized employee representative accompany the OSHA representative during an inspection tour
- to respond to questions from an OSHA inspector
- to review employer information about job-related accidents and injuries at the workplace
- participate in establishing standards
- be advised by their employer of hazards, prohibited by the law, that exist at the workplace and of possible exposure to toxic or dangerous materials
- be notified of any citations issued against their employer.

Some of the potential health hazards of jobs in which large numbers of women are employed are: organic solvents found in stencil machines, correction fluids, rubber cement, and ozone from copying machines (clerical workers); cotton dust, skin irritants, and chemicals (textile and apparel workers); hair, nail, and skin beauty preparations (hairdressers and beauticians); heat, heavy lifting, and chemicals (launderers and dry cleaners); solvents and acids (electronics workers); infectious diseases, heavy lifting, radiation, skin disorders, and anesthetic gases (hospital and other health care workers); and biological agents, flammable, explosive, toxic, or carcinogenic substances, exposure to radiation, and bites and allergies from research animals (laboratory workers).

Several cities and States have enacted laws requiring employers to inform their employees about toxic substances they are exposed to at the workplace. The National Labor Relations Board has also ruled that unions who request them must be given the names of chemicals and other substances the workers they represent are exposed to in the workplace.

Reports to OSHA from workers indicate that a number of major corporations are adopting or expanding policies that exclude women of childbearing age and pregnant women from jobs involving potential exposure to certain toxic substances because of possible fetal damage. Such policies may be a violation of the general duty clause of the Occupational Safety and Health Act. They may also violate title VII of the Civil Rights Act of 1964.

## What To Do

If you believe unsafe or unhealthful conditions exist in your workplace, you or your representative can file a complaint requesting an inspection. If there is a poster about the State or OSHA safety law at your workplace, your complaint should be filed with the indicated agency. If there is no poster, the complaint should be filed with OSHA (see Appendix B for address). OSHA will withhold names of complainants upon request. If you have been discharged or otherwise discriminated against in any way for exercising your rights under this law, you may file a discrimination complaint with OSHA within 30 days of the discriminatory action.

If you are concerned about the health effects of exposure to a given substance or working conditions, a request may be made to the National Institute for Occupational Safety and Health (NIOSH) to conduct a health hazard evaluation at your workplace.

A request for a health hazard evaluation should be addressed to NIOSH, Hazard Evaluation Services Branch, U.S. Department of Health and Human Services, Cincinnati, Ohio 45202.

## TERMINATION

There is no general law which prohibits private employers from discharging employees without good cause. Employers have historically had the right to fire employees at will, unless there was a written contract which protected against it. This broad right to discharge employees at will has been limited by a number of Federal laws which prohibit discrimination based on sex, race, color, religion, national origin, age, physical or mental handicap, union or other protected concerted activities, wage garnishment, and filing complaints or assisting in procedures related to enforcing these laws.

In addition, some States and municipalities have passed laws which prohibit discharge for serving on jury duty, filing workers' compensation claims, refusing to take lie detector tests, or for discrimination based on marital status or sexual orientation. Collective bargaining agreements between employers and unions, and employee complaint procedures, also impose limitations on the absolute right of an employer to fire workers.

Some employees have challenged their discharges in courts, and in a few cases have succeeded in placing additional limitations on employers' right to discharge. Courts in some States have ruled in favor of discharged employees — when the discharge was contrary to public policy, such as refusal to commit perjury or to approve market testing of a possibly harmful drug; when it was not based on good faith and fair dealing, such as discharge for refusal to date a supervisor, or to avoid paying a large commission; or when there was an implied promise of continued employment. An implied promise of continued employment might be demonstrated by the personnel policies or practices of an employer, an employee's length of service, the nature of the job, actions or communications by the employer, and industry practices.

# UNION PARTICIPATION AND OTHER PROTECTED ACTIVITIES

The National Labor Relations Act, as amended by the Labor-Management Relations Act, provides employees the right to form, join, or assist labor unions; to bargain collectively through representatives of their own choosing on wages, hours, and other terms of employment; and to engage in other concerted activities for the purpose of collective bargaining or other mutual aid or protection, such as striking to secure better working conditions. Employees are also guaranteed the right to refrain from membership or participation in a union, except where such membership is a requirement of employment. Laws in some States do not permit union membership to be a requirement of employment. Such laws are referred to as right-to-work laws. In the States where a union membership requirement is permitted, an employee usually has a grace period of not less than 30 days after being hired to become a member.

Certain labor practices by employers are labeled "unfair" and are prohibited by the NLRA. These include interference with or restraint or coercion of employees in the exercise of the rights described above; domination of or interference with the formation or administration of a labor organization, or the contribution of financial or other support to it; discrimination in hiring, tenure, or terms or conditions of employment in order to encourage or discourage membership in a labor organization; discharging or discriminating against an employee for filing charges or giving testimony under the act; and refusing to bargain collectively.

The law also defines unfair labor practices prohibited to unions. Unfair practices against workers include restraining them or coercing them in the exercise of their rights and requiring them to pay membership or initiation fees that are excessive or that discriminate between members. It is also an unfair practice for a union to cause an employer to discriminate against a worker. Maintaining separate locals for male and female employees is an example of the unfair practice of restraining and coercing employees in the exercise of their right to be represented by a representative of their choosing.

Some types of workers are exempt from the law. These include agricultural laborers, private household workers, independent contractors, supervisors, persons subject to the Railway Labor Act, public employees, and some hospital workers. For futher information write the nearest office of the National Labor Relations Board. A local post office can supply the address.

The Labor-Management Reporting and Disclosure Act (LMRDA) provides for the reporting and public disclosure of certain financial transactions and administrative practices for unions, union officers and employees, employers, labor relations consultants, and surety companies. It lays down a set of ground rules governing the use of union trusteeships and establishes democratic standards for union officer elections. It also establishes safeguards for the protection of union funds and property.

The LMRDA includes a Bill of Rights of members of labor organizations which protects their freedom of speech and assembly and their equal rights to nominate candidates for union office, vote in union elections and referendums, and attend and participate in membership meetings. It guarantees certain rights to union members facing discipline by labor organizations and establishes procedures which a labor organization must follow in increasing dues and initiation fees and imposing assessments. The LMRDA Bill of Rights establishes the right of an employee to review, or in some cases to obtain, a copy of each collective bargaining agreement directly affecting his or her rights as an employee.

The Department of Labor is responsible for enforcing some provisions of the LMRDA. Other provisions, however, are enforceable only through private suit by union members. For more information contact the Labor-Management Services Administration, U.S. Department of Labor, Washington, D.C. 20210.

## EMPLOYEE ACCESS TO PERSONNEL FILES

There is no Federal law which requires employers to allow employees to examine their own personnel files. However, in 1982, at least nine States had laws which required some or all employers to allow employees such access. Generally these laws do not cover items such as letters of reference or records relating to an investigation for a criminal offense.

Employees of the Federal civil service do have the right to inspect their personnel files. In addition, collective bargaining agreements between unions and employers may also provide for employee access, as may the personnel policies of individual employers.

## CHILD AND DEPENDENT CARE TAX CREDIT

A tax credit for actual expenses incurred for child or dependent care is available to an employed person if the expenditures enable that person to be gainfully employed. The credit is computed at 30 percent for taxpayers with incomes of $10,000 or less, with the rate of the credit reduced one percentage point for each additional $2,000 of income above $10,000. When incomes are over $28,000, the credit is computed at 20 percent. The limits on expenses for which the credit may be taken are $2,400 for one dependent and $4,800 for two or more dependents. The chart below shows the amount of credit that may be taken at various income levels.

The expenses may be for services provided in the taxpayer's home, or for out-of-home care for dependents under age 15, or for adult dependents who are disabled who live with the taxpayer. This means that day care expenses for dependent adults are included, but expenses for residential care in a nursing home or similar facility for dependent adults are not. Credit is available to all eligible taxpayers, regardless of the gross income of the family, whether or not they itemize deductions, or which tax form they file. It is available to married couples if either or both spouses work full and/or part time, to single working parents, and to full-time students with working spouses. To claim the credit, married couples must file a joint return. In the case of part-time workers, the amount of qualified expenses (those on which the 20 to 30 percent credit is figured) is limited to the earnings of the spouse with the lower income. For example, if one spouse earned less than $2,000 and the couple had two children, and the child care expenses exceeded $4,800, the amount of expenses allowable for computing the credit would be $2,000, the amount of the low-earning spouse's income. The earned income limit is equally applicable to unmarried taxpayers.

The credit is also available to a divorced or separated parent who has custody of a child under age 15 for more than half the calendar year — even though the other spouse may be entitled to claim the personal income tax exemption for a dependent child. A deserted spouse may claim the credit if the deserting spouse is absent for the last 6 months of the taxable year.

Payments to relatives, such as grandparents or adult children including those living in the same household, qualify for the credit, provided the relative is not the taxpayer's dependent and the relative's wages are subject to social security taxes. However, no credit is allowable for payments made to a child of the taxpayer under age 18.

The credit is computed on an annual basis. For that reason, the entire amount of qualifying expenses on which the credit is computed ($2,400 or $4,800) is available to eligible taxpayers having the appropriate number of dependents at any time during the taxable year.

| Family Income Before Taxes | Percentage Tax Credit | Maximum $ Amount of Credit | |
|---|---|---|---|
| | | 1 Dependent | 2 or More Dependents |
| Up to $10,000 | 30 | $720 | $1,440 |
| $10,001 to 12,000 | 29 | 696 | 1,392 |
| 12,001 to 14,000 | 28 | 672 | 1,344 |
| 14,001 to 16,000 | 27 | 648 | 1,296 |
| 16,001 to 18,000 | 26 | 624 | 1,248 |
| 18,001 to 20,000 | 25 | 600 | 1,200 |
| 20,001 to 22,000 | 24 | 576 | 1,152 |
| 22,001 to 24,000 | 23 | 552 | 1,104 |
| 24,001 to 26,000 | 22 | 528 | 1,056 |
| 26,001 to 28,000 | 21 | 504 | 1,008 |
| 28,001 and over | 20 | 480 | 960 |

The material in this chapter is taken from the U.S. Department of Labor pamphlet "A Working Woman's Guide to Her Job Rights." It was prepared by Ruth Robinson and Jane Walstedt.

# APPENDIX B

## SOURCES OF ASSISTANCE
## FEDERAL AGENCIES

### National Offices

U.S. Equal Employment
Opportunity Commission
Washington, D.C. 20506
(See also list of field
offices following.)

Civil Rights Division
U.S. Department of Health
and Human Services
Washington, D.C. 20201

Social Security Administration
U.S. Department of Health
and Human Services
Baltimore, Maryland 21235

Internal Revenue Service
U.S. Department of the Treasury
Washington, D.C. 20224

Office of Revenue Sharing
U.S. Department of the Treasury
Washington, D.C. 20226

Federal Trade Commission
Washington, D.C. 20580

Pension Benefit Guaranty Corp.
2020 K Street, NW.
Washington, D.C. 20006

Labor-Management Services
Administration
U.S. Department of Labor
Washington, D.C. 20216

Occupational Safety and
Health Administration
U.S. Department of Labor
Washington, D.C. 20210

Office of Federal Contract
Compliance Programs
Employment Standards
Administration
U.S. Department of Labor
Washington, D.C. 20210
(See also list of regional offices
following.)

Office of Workers'
Compensation Programs
Employment Standards
Administration
U.S. Department of Labor
Washington, D.C. 20210

Women's Bureau
Office of the Secretary
U.S. Department of Labor
Washington, D.C. 20210

Wage and Hour Division
Employment Standards
Administration
U.S. Department of Labor
Washington, D.C. 20210
(See also list of field offices
following.)

### Equal Employment Opportunity Commission (EEOC) Field Offices

**Albuquerque:** 505 Marquette,
NW., Suite 1515, New Mexico 87101

**Atlanta:** 75 Piedmont Avenue,
NE., 10th Floor, Georgia 30303

**Baltimore:** 711 West 40th Street,
Suite 210, Maryland 21211

**Birmingham:** 2121 Eighth Avenue,
North, Alabama 35203

**Boston:** 150 Causeway Street, Suite
1000, Massachusetts 02114

**Buffalo:** One West Genesee Street,
Room 320, New York, 14202

**Charlotte:** 1301 East Morehead,
North Carolina 28204

**Chicago:** 536 South Clark Street,
Room 234, Illinois 60605

**Cincinnati:** 550 Main Street, Room 7019, Ohio 45202

**Cleveland:** 1365 Ontario Street, Room 602, Ohio 44114

**Dallas:** 1900 Pacific, 13th Floor, Texas 75201

**Dayton:** 200 West Second Street, Room 608, Ohio 45402

**Denver:** 1513 Stout Street, 6th Floor, Colorado 80202

**Detroit:** 660 Woodward Avenue, Suite 600, Michigan 48226

**El Paso:** 2211 East Missouri, Room E-235, Texas 79903

**Fresno:** 1313 P Street, Suite 103, California 93721

**Greensboro:** 324 West Market Street, Room 132, North Carolina 27402

**Greenville:** 7 North Laurens Street, Suite 507, South Carolina 29602

**Houston:** 2320 LaBranch, Room 1101, Texas 77004

**Indianapolis:** 46 East Ohio Street, Room 456, Indiana 46204

**Jackson:** 100 West Capitol Street, Suite 721, Mississippi 39201

**Kansas City:** 1150 Grand, 1st Foor, Missouri 64106

**Little Rock:** 700 West Capitol, Arkansas 72201

**Los Angeles:** 3255 Wilshire Boulevard, 9th Floor, California 90010

**Louisville:** 600 Jefferson Street, Kentucky 40202

**Memphis:** 1407 Union Avenue, Suite 502, Tennessee 38104

**Miami:** 300 Biscayne Boulevard Way, Suite 414, Florida 33131

**Milwaukee:** 342 North Water Street, Room 612, Wisconsin 53202

**Minneapolis:** 12 South Sixth Street, Minnesota 55402

**Nashville:** 404 James Robertson Parkway, Suite 1822, Tennessee 37219

**Newark:** 744 Broad Street, Room 502, New Jersey 07102

**New Orleans:** 600 South Street, Louisiana 70130

**New York:** 90 Church Street, Room 1301, New York 10007

**Norfolk:** 200 Granby Mall, Room 412, Virginia 23510

**Oakland:** 1515 Clay Street, Room 640, California 94612

**Oklahoma City:** 50 Penn Place, Suite 1430, Oklahoma 73118

**Philadelphia:** 127 North Fourth Street, Suite 200, Pennsylvania 19106

**Phoenix:** 201 North Central Avenue, Suite 1450, Arizona 85073

**Pittsburgh:** 1000 Liberty Avenue, Room 2038A, Pennsylvania 15222

**Raleigh:** 414 Fayetteville Street, North Carolina 27608

**Richmond:** 400 North Eighth Street, Room 6213, Virginia 23240

**San Antonio:** 727 East Durango, Suite B-601, Texas 78206

**San Diego:** 880 Front Street, California 92188

**San Francisco:** 1390 Market Street, Suite 325, California 94102

**San Jose:** 84 West Santa Clara Avenue, Room 300, California 95113

**Seattle:** 710 Second Avenue, 7th Floor, Washington 98104

**St. Louis:** 625 North Euclid Street, Missouri 63108

**Tampa:** 700 Twiggs Street, Room 302, Florida 33602

**Washington:** 1717 H Street, NW., Suite 402, District of Columbia 20006

## Office of Federal Contract Compliance Programs (OFCCP) Regional and Area Offices

Addresses and telephone numbers for area offices are listed in the telephone directory under "United States Department of Labor."

**Boston:** U.S. Department of Labor, JFK Building, Room 1612-C, Government Center, Massachusetts 02203. *Bridgeport, Hartford, Providence.*

**New York:** U.S. Department of Labor, 1515 Broadway, Room 338, New York 10036. *Albany, Buffalo, Garden City, Newark, San Juan, Syracuse, Trenton, White Plains.*

**Philadelphia:** U.S. Department of Labor, Gateway Building, Room 1310, 3535 Market Street, Pennsylvania 19104. *Baltimore, Pittsburgh, Reading, Richmond, Washington.*

**Atlanta:** U.S. Department of Labor, 1371 Peachtree Street, NE., Room 111, Georgia 30309. *Birmingham, Charlotte, Columbia, Jackson, Jacksonville, Louisville, Memphis, Miami, Nashville, Orlando, Raleigh.*

**Chicago:** U.S. Department of Labor, New Federal Building, Room 3910, 320 South Dearborn Street, Illinois 60604. *Cleveland, Columbus, Detroit, Gary, Grand Rapids, Indianapolis, Milwaukee, Minneapolis, Peoria.*

**Dallas:** U.S. Department of Labor, 555 Griffin Square Building, Room 505, Texas 75202. *Albuquerque, Ft. Worth, Houston, Little Rock, New Orleans, San Antonio, Tulsa*

**Kansas City:** U.S. Department of Labor, Federal Office Building, Room 2000, 911 Walnut Street, Missouri 64106. *St. Louis, Omaha.*

**Denver:** U.S. Department of Labor, 1412 Federal Office Building, 1961 Stout Street, Colorado 80294. *Salt Lake City.*

**San Francisco:** U.S. Department of Labor, 450 Golden Gate Avenue, Room 11435, California 94102. *Honolulu, Los Angeles, Oakland, Phoenix, Santa Ana, San Diego, San Jose, Van Nuys.*

**Seattle:** U.S. Department of Labor, Federal Office Building, 909 First Avenue, Room 3088, Washington 98174, *Anchorage, Portland.*

## Wage and Hour Division

Inquiries about laws administered by the Wage and Hour Division, U.S. Department of Labor, should be addressed to the nearest office. Consult the list below. Offices shown in italics are staffed by investigative personnel whose duties frequently require them to be away from the office. Telephone messages and requests for information may be left at these offices when investigators are not on duty at the office. Personal appointments may be made by either telephone or mail.

**Alabama:** *Anniston,* Birmingham, *Cullman, Dotha, Florence, Gadsden, Huntsville,* Mobile, Montgomery, *Opelika, Selma, Tuscaloosa*

**Alaska:** *Anchorage*

**Arizona:** Phoenix, *Tucson*

**Arkansas:** *El Dorado, Fort Smith, Jonesboro,* Little Rock, *Pine Bluff*

**California:** *Fresno,* Glendale, *Laguna Niquel, Long Beach,* Los Angeles, *Modesto, Oakland, Oxnard,* Sacramento, *Salinas, San Bernardino, San Diego,* San Francisco, *San Jose,* Santa Ana

**Colorado:** *Colorado Springs,* Denver, *Ft. Collins, Grand Junction, Pueblo*

**Connecticut:** *Bridgeport,* Hartford, *New London*

**Delaware:** *Dover, Wilmington*

**District of Columbia:** Hyattsville (Md.)

**Florida:** *Clearwater, Cocoa Beach, Daytona Beach,* Fort Lauderdale, *Fort Myers, Gainesville, Homestead,* Jacksonville, *Lakeland, Leesburg, Melbourne, Miami, Orlando,* Panama City, Pensacola, St. Petersburg, Sarasota, Tallahassee, Tampa, *West Palm Beach*

**Georgia:** *Albany, Athens,* Atlanta, *Augusta, Brunswick,* Columbus, *Gainesville, Macon, Marietta, Rome,* Savannah, Thomasville, Waycross

**Hawaii:** Honolulu

**Idaho:** *Boise*

**Illinois:** *Belleville, Champaign,* Chicago, *Elgin, Geneva, Gurnee, Marion, Peoria, Rockford, Rock Island,* Springfield

**Indiana:** *Anderson, Evansville, Fort Wayne, Gary,* Indianapolis, *Lafayette, Marion, New Albany,* South Bend, Terre Haute

**Iowa:** *Burlington, Cedar Rapids, Davenport, Des Moines,* Sioux City

**Kansas:** *Pittsburg, Salina,* Wichita

**Kentucky:** *Ashland, Bowling Green, Covington, Elizabethtown,* Lexington, Louisville, *Middlesboro,* Owensboro

**Louisiana:** Baton Rouge, *Lafayette, Lake Charles, Monroe,* New Orleans, *Shreveport*

**Maine:** *Bangor,* Portland

**Maryland:** Baltimore, *Hagerstown,* Hyattsville, *Salisbury*

**Massachusetts:** Boston, *Brockton,* Springfield

**Michigan:** Detroit, *Escanaba, Flint,* Grand Rapids, *Kalamazoo, Lansing, Pontiac, Port Huron, Saginaw,* Troy

**Minnesota:** *Brainerd, Duluth, Mankato,* Minneapolis

**Mississippi:** *Biloxi, Columbus, Greenville, Greenwood, Hattiesburg,* Jackson, *Meridian, Tupelo*

**Missouri:** *Cape Girardeau, Joplin,* Kansas City, St. Louis, *Springfield*

**Montana:** *Billings, Great Falls, Missoula*

**Nebraska:** *Lincoln,* Omaha, *Scottsbluff*

**Nevada:** *Las Vegas, Reno*

**New Hampshire:** *Manchester*

**New Jersey:** *Atlantic City, Camden,* Newark, *Paterson,* Trenton

**New Mexico:** Albuquerque, *Las Cruces, Roswell*

**New York:** Albany, Binghamton, Bronx, Brooklyn, Buffalo, Hempstead, *Newburgh,* New York, *Poughkeepsie,* Rochester, *Syracuse*

**North Carolina:** *Asheville,* Charlotte, *Durham, Fayetteville, Gastonia, Goldsboro, Greenville,* Greensboro, *Hickory, New Bern,* Raleigh, *Salisbury, Wilmington, Winston-Salem*

**North Dakota:** *Bismarck, Fargo*

**Ohio:** Akron, *Cambridge, Canton,* Cincinnati, Cleveland, Columbus, *Dayton, Lima, Mansfield, Middletown, Toledo, The Plains, Youngstown, Sandusky*

**Oklahoma:** *Ardmore, Enid, Lawton, Muskogee,* Oklahoma City, Tulsa

**Oregon:** *Eugene, Medford,* Portland

**Pennsylvania:** *Allentown, Altoona, Erie, Greensburg,* Harrisburg, *Indiana, Johnstown, Lancaster,* Philadelphia, Pittsburgh, *Reading, Scranton, Uniontown, Washington,* Wilkes Barre, *Williamsport, York*

**Puerto Rico:** *Arecibo,* Hato Rey, *Mayaguez,* Ponce

**Rhode Island:** *Providence*

**South Carolina:** *Charleston,* Columbia, *Florence, Greenville, Spartanburg*

**South Dakota:** *Rapid City, Sioux Falls*

**Tennessee:** *Bristol, Chattanooga, Columbia, Cookeville, Harrison,* Jackson, *Johnson City,* Knoxville, *Memphis,* Nashville, *Union City*

**Texas:** *Abilene, Amarillo, Austin, Beaumont, Brownsville, Bryon,* Corpus Christi, Dallas, Fort Worth, *Galveston, Harlingen,* Houston, *Laredo, Longview, Lubbock, Lufkin, McAllen, San Angelo,* San Antonio, *Sherman, Texarkana, Tyler, Victoria, Waco, Wichita Falls*

**Utah:** *Ogden, Provo,* Salt Lake City

**Vermont:** *Burlington*

**Virginia:** *Danville, Falls Church, Lynchburg, Norfolk,* Richmond, *Roanoke, Waynesboro, Winchester*

**Washington:** *Everett,* Seattle, *Spokane, Tacoma, Yakima*

**West Virginia:** *Beckley, Bridgeport,* Charleston, *Huntington, Parkersburg, Wheeling*

**Wisconsin:** *Eau Claire, Green Bay, La Crosse,* Madison, Milwaukee, *Oshkosh, Racine, Wausau*

**Wyoming:** *Casper*

# APPENDIX C

## STATE AGENCIES
### Labor Departments and Human Rights Commissions

**Alabama:** Department of Industrial Relations, Industrial Relations Building, Montgomery, 36130.

**Alaska:** Department of Labor, P.O. Box 1149, Juneau, 99811. Alaska State Commission for Human Rights, 431 W. 7th Ave., Suite 105, Anchorage, 99501.

**Arizona:** Department of Labor, 1601 West Jefferson Street, P.O. Box 19070, Phoenix, 85001. Arizona Civil Rights Division, 1275 W. Washington, Phoenix, 85001.

**Arkansas:** Department of Labor, 1022 High Street, Little Rock, 72202.

**California:** Department of Industrial Relations, 525 Golden Gate Avenue, P.O. Box 603, San Francisco, 94101. Department of Fair Employment and Housing, 1201 I Street, Sacramento, 95814.

**Colorado:** Department of Labor and Employment, 251 East 12th Avenue, Denver, 80203. Colorado Civil Rights Commission, State Services Building, 1525 Sherman Street, Denver, 80203.

**Connecticut:** State Board of Labor Relations, 2000 Folly Brook Boulevard, Wethersfield, 06109. Commission on Human Rights and Opportunities, 90 Washington Street, Hartford, 06115.

**Delaware:** Department of Labor and Industrial Relations, 820 N. French Street, Wilmington, 19801. (Includes Anti-Discrimination Section.)

**District of Columbia:** D.C. Department of Employment Services, 500 C Street, NW., Washington, D.C. 20001. Commission on Human Rights, 1424 K Street, NW., Washington, D.C. 20004.

**Florida:** Industrial Relations Commission, Berkeley Building, 2562 Executive Center Circle East, Tallahassee, 32301. Commission on Human Relations, Montgomery Building, 2562 Executive Center Circle East, Tallahassee, 32301.

**Georgia:** Department of Labor, State Labor Building, 254 Washington Street, SW., Atlanta, 30334.

**Guam:** Department of Labor, Government of Guam, Box 23548, GMF, Guam, M.I. 96921.

**Hawaii:** Department of Labor and Industrial Relations, 825 Mililani Street, Honolulu, 96813.

**Idaho:** Department of Labor and Industrial Services, Industrial Administration Building, 317 Main Street, Boise, 83720. Commission on Human Rights, Statehouse, Boise, 83720.

**Illinois:** Department of Labor, 910 South Michigan Avenue, Chicago, 60605. Department of Human Rights, 32 West Randolph Street, Chicago, 60601.

**Indiana:** Division of Labor, Room 1013, Indiana State Office Building, 100 N. Senate Avenue, Indianapolis, 46204. Civil Rights Commission, 311 West Washington Street, Indianapolis, 46204.

**Iowa:** Bureau of Labor, 307 East 7th Street, Des Moines, 50319. Civil Rights Commission, 8th Floor, Colony Building, 507 Tenth Street, Des Moines, 50319.

**Kansas:** Department of Human Resources, Division of Labor Management and Labor Standards, 512 West 6th Street, Topeka, 66603. Commission on Civil Rights, 535 Kansas Avenue, 5th Floor, Topeka, 66603.

**Kentucky:** Department of Labor, U.S. 127 South, Frankfort, 40601. Commission on Human Rights, 823 Capital Plaza Tower, Frankfort, 40601.

**Louisiana:** Department of Labor, 1045 Natural Resources Building, P.O. Box 44063, Baton Rouge, 70804.

**Maine:** Bureau of Labor Standards, 7th Floor, State Office Building, Augusta, 04333. Human Rights Commission, State House — Station 51, Augusta, 04333.

**Maryland:** Division of Labor and Industry, 203 East Baltimore Street, Baltimore, 21202. Commission on Human Relations, 20 East Franklin Street, Baltimore, 21202.

**Massachusetts:** Department of Labor and Industries, State Office Building, 100 Cambridge Street, Boston 02202. Commission Against Discrimination, 1 Ashburton Place, Suite 601, Boston, 02108

**Michigan:** Department of Labor, Leonard Plaza Building, 309 N. Washington, P.O. Box 30015, Lansing, 48909. Department of Civil Rights, Billie Farnum Building, 125 W. Allegan Street, Lansing, 48913.

**Minnesota:** Department of Labor and Industry, 444 Lafayette Road, St. Paul, 55101. Department of Human Rights, 5th Floor Bremer Tower, 7th Place and Minnesota Street, St. Paul, 55101.

**Mississippi:** Employment Security Commission, 1520 West Capitol, P.O. Box 1699, Jackson, 39205.

**Missouri:** Department of Labor and Industrial Relations, 1904 Missouri Boulevard, P.O. Box 599, Jefferson City, 65102.

**Montana:** Department of Labor and Industry, Capital Station, Helena, 59620. Human Rights Commission, 23 South Last Chance Gulch, Helena, 59620.

**Nebraska:** Department of Labor, 550 S. 16th Street, Box 94600, State House Station, Lincoln, 68509. Equal Opportunity Commission, 301 Centennial Mall South, P.O. Box 94934, Lincoln, 68509.

**Nevada:** State Labor Commission, Capitol Complex, 505 East King Street, Carson City, 89710. Equal Rights Commission, 1515 E. Tropicana, Las Vegas, 89158.

**New Hampshire:** Department of Labor, 19 Pillsbury Street, Concord, 03301. Commission for Human Rights, 61 South Spring Street, Concord, 03301.

**New Jersey:** Department of Labor, CN 110, Trenton, 08625. Division on Civil Rights, 1100 Raymond Boulevard, Newark, 07102.

**New Mexico:** State Labor and Industrial Commission, 509 Camino de Los Marquez, Santa Fe, 87501. Human Rights Commission, 303 Bataan Memorial Building, Santa Fe, 87503.

**New York:** Department of Labor, State Campus, Albany, 12240. Division of Human Rights, Two World Trade Center, New York City, 10047.

**North Carolina:** Department of Labor, Labor Building, 4 W. Edenton Street, Raleigh, 27601.

**North Dakota:** Department of Labor, State Capitol, Bismarck, 58505.

**Ohio:** Department of Industrial Relations, 2323 W. 5th Avenue, Columbus, 43216. Civil Rights Commission, 220 Parsons Avenue, Columbus, 43215.

**Oklahoma:** Department of Labor, State Capitol Building, Suite 118, Oklahoma City, 73105. Human Rights Commission, Room G11, Jim Thorpe Building, P.O. Box 52945, Oklahoma City, 73152.

**Oregon:** Bureau of Labor and Industries, State Office Building, 1400 SW. Fifth Avenue, Portland, 97201. (Includes Civil Rights Division.)

**Pennsylvania:** Department of Labor and Industry, 1700 Labor and Industry Building, Harrisburg, 17120. Human Relations Commission, 101 South Second Street, Suite 300, P.O. Box 3145, Harrisburg, 17105.

**Puerto Rico:** Department of Labor, 505 Munoz Rivera Avenue, Hato Rey, 00918. (Includes Anti-Discrimination Unit.)

**Rhode Island:** Department of Labor, 220 Elmwood Avenue, Providence, 02907. Commission for Human Rights, 334 Westminster Mall, Providence, 02903.

**South Carolina:** Department of Labor, 3600 Forest Drive, P.O. Box 11329, Columbia, 29211. Human Affairs Commission, Post Office Drawer 11300, Columbia, 29211.

**South Dakota:** Department of Labor, Capitol Complex, 700 Illinois North, Pierre 57501. Commission on Human Rights, State Capitol Building, Pierre, 57501.

**Tennessee:** Department of Labor, 501 Union Building, Nashville, 37219. Commission for Human Development, 208 Tennessee Building, 535 Church Street, Nashville, 37219.

**Texas:** Department of Labor and Standards, P.O. Box 12157, Capitol Station, Austin, 78711.

**Utah:** Industrial Commission, 560 South 300 East, Salt Lake City, 84111. Anti-Discrimination Division, 560 South 300 East, Salt Lake City, 84111.

**Vermont:** Department of Labor and Industry, State Office Building, Montpelier, 05602.

**Virginia:** Department of Labor and Industry, 205 N. 4th Street, P.O. Box 12064, Richmond, 23214.

**Virgin Islands:** Department of Labor, P.O. Box 890, Christiansted, St. Croix, 00820.

**Washington:** Department of Labor and Industries, General Administration Building, Olympia, 98504. Human Rights Commission, 402 Evergreen Plaza Building, FJ-41, Olympia, 98504.

**West Virginia:** Department of Labor, Capitol Complex, 1900 Washington Street East, Charleston, 25305. Human Rights Commission, 215 Professional Building, 1036 Quarrier Street, Charleston, 25301.

**Wisconsin:** Department of Industry, Labor and Human Relations, 201 East Washington Avenue, P.O. Box 7946, Madison, 53707. Equal Rights Division, P.O. Box 7903, Madison, 53707.

**Wyoming:** Department of Labor and Statistics, Hathaway Building, Cheyenne, 82002. Fair Employment Practices Commission, Hathaway Building, Cheyenne, 82002.

30853